A New Day

By

Rev. Msgr. Chester P. Michael S.T.D.

Copyright © 2011 by Chester P. Michael

ISBN 0-7414-6272-9

Printed in the United States of America

Published March 2011

INFINITY PUBLISHING
1094 New DeHaven Street, Suite 100
West Conshohocken, PA 19428-2713
Toll-free (877) BUY BOOK
Local Phone (610) 941-9999
Fax (610) 941-9959
Info@buybooksontheweb.com
www.buybooksontheweb.com

Table of Contents

ACKNOWLEDGMENTS

Many persons have contributed to the writing and publishing of this book. Marie Norrisey has given many, many long hours to the editing of the manuscript. Beverly Vandevender typed the first edition of this book. Betty Jane Hagen, Karin Ewan and Gregg Kendrick created the second edition. Betty Jane Hagen, Julie Hendrick and Connie Porter wrote the suggested questions for discussion at the end of each chapter.

INTRODUCTION

Every day is a new day; every period of history is a new day. Whether it will be a good new day or a bad new day depends upon how well we cooperate with the graces and blessings God bestows upon us. God wants every day to be a good day. God gives us the needed assistance to make every day a good day. But having given human beings the gift of freedom, God's hands are somewhat tied and limited. We need to use our freedom to cooperate with God's daily graces. If we fail to do so, or choose to use our freedom to rebel against God's plans for us, a new day becomes an evil day for us as well as for those dependent upon us.

Some new days are more important than others. Some periods of history have greater influence on the future than other historical periods. Today we seem to be living in one of those more important periods of history. The decisions we make from day to day will have tremendous influence on the whole future of the human race. It would seem that we are at the cutting edge of the future destiny of the world. The so-called modern world is fast becoming a thing of the past. Whether we like to use the term "new age" or not, it seems clear that a whole new era of history is facing us. Many people connect this new era with the third Christian millennium.

Regardless of how we look at the future, there is general agreement that the decisions each of us is making each day will determine the direction the human race will take. We seem to be in a similar situation to that described in Chapter 18 of the Book of Genesis. God tells Abraham, "The outcry against Sodom and Gomorrah is so great, and their sin so grave, that I must go down and see whether or not their actions fully correspond to the cry against them that comes to me." Abraham had relatives in these sinful cities, so he pleads with God to spare the cities. "Please, let not my Lord grow angry if I speak up this last time. What if there are at least ten just persons there?" The Lord replied, "For the sake of those ten, I will not destroy it."

The evil and violence in today's world is comparable to the evil of Sodom and Gomorrah. It will probably take more than ten good persons to prevent the destruction of our present sinful world which is a million times larger than Sodom and Gomorrah. But the principle still holds true that a few good persons can change the future destiny of our world. The fewer we are, the more whole and holy we need to be. Therefore, instead of wringing our hands in frustration at the sight of so much evil in today's world, each of us is called and challenged to do all in our power to make the new day now facing us a good day.

The thing that makes our present age so difficult is what we might call "institutional evil." Evil has become endemic in nearly all the institutions of today's world. Our civil governments, our churches, our large industrial corporations, our military establishment, our news media, our entertainment industries are all contaminated by a worship of power, pleasure and possessions. These "three P's" are all creations of God and therefore good. But they are only a limited good. When individuals or institutions make one or more of them into absolute goods, we divinize them and turn them into idols which we worship. Thus we become guilty of idolatry. These "three P's" are what traditionally have been called the world (possessions), the flesh (pleasure) and the devil (power).

An example of the power of institutional evil is seen in the acceptance of abortion and pro-choice by the great majority of our American citizens today. Since the Supreme Court and our civil government have declared that it is legal to destroy the human life of unborn children, most Americans accept this evil choice as legitimate and in accord with justice and right doing. Something similar occurred in Germany during the Nazi regime when practically the whole German nation approved of the elimination of the Jewish people living in their midst.

The worship of power, pleasure and possessions has become so ingrained in the lives of individuals as well as most of our institutions that it has become a form of satanic possession. These "three P's" that are gifts of God when used within proper limits, become evil forces (demons) when we turn them into absolute, unlimited goods. We become addicted or excessively attached to them. We become obsessed or possessed by them. They now become the gods whom we worship and obey rather than the true God. This is exactly the meaning of demonic possession.

If the future of the world is to be a good new day, we must find a way to exorcise these evil spirits (powers) which now possess so much of our society. The three traditional remedies for exorcising these evils are prayer, fasting and almsgiving. Prayer gives to God absolute power over us and prevents us from making the power of our free will into an absolute good. Fasting enables us to bring under control our excessive attachments to pleasure. Almsgiving encourages us to share our goods with others and thus prevent possessions from becoming an absolute good.

Besides the personal efforts of prayer, fasting and almsgiving, we need special help from God. Traditionally this divine help comes to us in the form of faith, hope and charity. Through these God-given graces we are able to attain the unconditional love that will exorcise and rid us of our obsessive attachment to power, pleasure and possessions. Unconditional love is present when we are able consistently to put the needs of God and others ahead of our own selfish desires.

In this book I shall try to expand upon all the above ideas in order to give the reader a workable plan for the new day that is now facing us. I will use the two terms "nature" and "grace" to distinguish between those gifts of God which naturally belong to us as human beings and the special helps from God which come to us through the sacraments and the Incarnation of God in Jesus Christ. Tradition holds that "grace builds on nature." I will first discuss the natural helps God has given us to overcome evil and then show how God's special graces build on our natural maturity. The goal is both a natural wholeness and a supernatural, Christ-like sanctity. Leon Bloy, a French novelist and poet of the late 19th and early 20th century, once remarked, "The only tragedy is the failure to become a saint." Saints have always been needed in the history of the world and God has provided us with saintly examples of virtue in every generation. Today, perhaps more than any other period of world history, the human race needs a number of saints to prevent the modern world from going the way of Sodom and Gomorrah.

Throughout this book I use the terms 'first aeon,' 'second aeon,' and 'third aeon.' The final chapter is entitled *Third Aeon – Goal of Divine Love.* Aeon refers to a period of time. The first aeon is that period of time from creation of the world until the Incarnation of Jesus two thousand years ago. The second aeon began with the Incarnation of Jesus in the womb of Mary and will continue until the final coming of Jesus at the end of the present world. The third aeon actually began with the resurrection of Jesus on Easter but will be fully present only after our death and with the final coming of Jesus. It will continue for all eternity.

There will be a bit of confusion in the use of gender regarding God. Traditionally, we have been accustomed to speak of God as masculine. This is the gender used for God in both the Old and New Testaments. In recent years we have tried to remedy this patriarchal attitude towards God by speaking of God as mother as well as father. In the only public address by Pope John Paul I during his thirty days as pope, he insisted that God is both mother and father. He quoted from the Book of Isaiah, Chapters 49 and 66, as proof of the feminine side of God. For the most part in this book I have tried to resolve this gender issue by referring to God as "He/She" or "S/He." Some people will find this a bit awkward and confusing. I apologize for the confusion. Please use the term with which you feel most comfortable.

This edition of *A New Day* is somewhat different from the first 1999 edition. I have added five new chapters, eliminated Chapter fourteen and shifted Chapter eleven to the end of the book.

CHAPTER 1

A New Day

"In the beginning God created the heavens and the earth; the earth was waste and void; darkness covered the abyss and the Spirit of God was stirring above the waters. God said, 'Let there be light,' and there was light. God saw that the light was good. God separated the light from the darkness, calling the light Day and the darkness Night. And there was evening and morning the first day" (Gn 1:1-5). God began His/Her creation with a new day, filled with light, peace and joy. But sin entered the world and darkness covered the earth for a long time.

With the age of Abraham, dawn began to appear in the skies. Isaiah and the other prophets spoke of a great new day of the Lord that would soon come. "The people who walked in darkness have seen a great light; upon those who dwelt in the land of gloom, a light has shone. You have brought them abundant joy and great rejoicing ... for a child is born to us, a son is given us ... his dominion is vast and forever peaceful" (Is 9:2-6).

The Gospels tell us that the prophecy of Isaiah was fulfilled with the advent of Christ, the light of the world (Mt 4:16). "In him was life and the life was the light of men. And the light shines in the darkness and the darkness grasped it not" (Jn 1:4-5). For a brief while the light of this new day shone brightly upon the earth. "I have come a light into the world that whoever believes in me may not remain in darkness" (Jn 12:46). Then evil once again overcame the light. "This is your hour and the power of darkness" (Lk 22:53). However, on this occasion the victory of darkness over light was only an apparent one. "Late in the night of the Sabbath, as the first day of the week began to dawn ... an angel of the Lord came down from heaven ... his countenance was like lightning and his raiment like snow ... The angel spoke and said to the women, 'Do not be afraid; for I know that you seek Jesus who was crucified. He is not here for he has risen even as he said'" (Mt 28:1-6).

With the resurrection of Christ, another new day had dawned upon the world. Since that time we have been able to walk in the light of the risen Christ. Each day that has been given us during the intervening centuries has been a new day of grace. Though at times evening has come and we have experienced darkness for a while, we believe that never again will the darkness of sin overcome the light of God's grace, bestowed on us through Jesus Christ. Each morning we are able to start afresh with new grace and courage. Each Eucharist we celebrate is a new day of grace, a new union with Christ. No matter how many years we live in this present aeon, there is always something refreshing about each new day. God never repeats Him/Herself; each dawn we are able to rise to some surprise our Lord has reserved to give us at this particular moment. Provided we do our best to cooperate with these new graces, there should never be an occasion when we grow tired of God or religion. If the thought of the future does not fill us with enthusiasm and the joy of anticipation, then somehow we are failing to use the grace that has been given us. Every day should be a day of growth toward wholeness and sanctity. There will be many ups and downs along this path to maturity and sanctity, but if we are faithful, grace and love will burn ever brighter and brighter in our lives.

From time to time during the course of the centuries, there has risen exceedingly luminous periods of grace. We of this generation could be seeing one of these times. Pope John XXIII prayed for a new Pentecost in our time, a new outpouring of God's Holy Spirit upon the earth. We could be experiencing today a greater manifestation of God's love than any other age of Christianity. Both in secular and religious fields the world is making tremendous advances in knowledge. The extraordinary light of truth that has been given us demands that we correspond with it and work to make our age one of great grace for all generations to come.

On the other hand, we see many serious threats to the present and future welfare of the world, the church and our own country. The worship of the "three P's" of Power, Pleasure and Possessions contaminates nearly all our institutions as well as the lives of many people. The threat of disaster to our whole planetary environment is very real. The tremendous increase of world population presents us with a problem which so far we have been unable to solve. The distance between the "haves" and the "have-nots" of the world becomes greater each year. Racial and ethnic violence poses a constant threat to the present and future welfare of the human race. The streets of our cities and the halls of our schools become more and more dangerous to life and property. Alcoholism and drug addiction become more and more prevalent. All these dangers give us added incentive to go all out in leading the world toward good rather than allow evil and fear to throw the progress of the world backward for a tremendous loss.

None of us can afford to be mediocre. We are all called to be saints according to the state of life God has destined for us, and to bear witness to the truth of Christ with the shining light of a life of total dedication to God. We all can be dedicated apostles in bringing the message of salvation to our sisters and brothers. Having received so much light and love, we must not be satisfied until we have shared our riches with the whole world. It is the will of God that all humanity be joined into the one great family of Christ. A martyr is one who bears witness to truth with one's whole life and, when necessary, with death. In our age we need a great army of martyrs who are so sure of the value of the good news of Christ that they will gladly give their lives for its sake.

Let no one complain that there is nothing to do. There are immense tasks awaiting each of us. The great synthesis of the physical and spiritual, the natural and the supernatural, so needed today, will require the combined efforts of many minds and many hands. Divine providence has given our present age the task of striking a balance between nature and grace, individual and community, femininity and masculinity, body and soul, God and humanity. We have been given the light to see both sides of the truth at the same time. We have the gigantic task of formulating the many laws that govern the delicate balance between these extremes. This is especially necessary in the field of human and divine love which is at present so prominent in the thoughts and desires of the human race. With the advent of depth psychology, we have discovered a whole new world of love, and now, like Christopher Columbus, it is our task to find the best routes to these new lands. We must also find a way of uniting the old cultures with the new, and so lay the foundations of another age of the world that could be more glorious than any of the past. What a joy it can be for us to work, preparing the way for those who will come after us.

All of life should be progress toward the day when Christ will establish the Kingdom of God in its fullness. On that, the greatest of all days, everything will sparkle with the brightness of a renewed creation. Truth and love will reign supreme upon the earth. The darkness of error and the coldness of hate will be banished forever. The Lord will separate the wheat from the cockle which, until now, have been allowed to grow side by side. Separated forever from all evil, the good will be able to enjoy an everlasting life of love in the Kingdom of God. "I saw a new heaven and a new earth. For the first heaven and first earth passed away. And I saw

the holy city, the New Jerusalem, coming down out of heaven from God, made ready as a bride adorned for her husband. And I heard a loud voice from the throne saying,
'Behold the dwelling of God with people. S/He will dwell
with them and they will be His/Her people and God
Him/Herself will be with them as their God. And God will
wipe away every tear from their eyes. And death will be no
more, neither shall there be mourning nor crying nor pain
any more, for the former things have passed away.' And
S/He who was sitting on the throne said, 'Behold, I make all
things new'" (Rev 21:1-5).

This promise of God at the very conclusion of the last book
of the Bible will surely one day be fulfilled. However, our
Lord assures us that we know neither the day nor the hour
when it will be accomplished. We are reminded that our human cooperation or our failure to cooperate will somehow
affect the final outcome. In other words, we have the power
either to hasten or delay the final Day of the Lord. For example, if through our failure to pray and work for peace, a
worldwide nuclear war or holocaust should result, we could
be responsible for throwing back many thousands of years
God's time table for the Day of the Lord.

It would seem from a close reading of the words of Jesus in
the Gospels, that two thousand years ago, God was ready to
establish the Kingdom of God on earth. However, because
the people of that time failed to listen to Jesus, God's plans
for the Kingdom had to be delayed. It is also possible that
every generation since the time of Christ has been given the
grace and opportunity to establish that Kingdom of God so
long desired by God and humankind. However, there are
special times of grace when the possibility of establishing the
Kingdom of God is more present than others. Today seems
to be such a time. How then can we make a really worthwhile contribution to the Kingdom of God? Primarily, it will

be accomplished by our day-to-day growth in wholeness and sanctity.

An example of the power of just one human being to change the course of history is that of St. Nicholas of Flue, patron saint of Switzerland. He was a farmer, politician and father of ten children who then became a hermit. He spent many years as a hermit dispensing advice to all who came to him. In 1481 when the quarrelling Swiss cantons were on the verge of civil war, "Brother Klaus" as he was affectionately called, was able to bring peace to the whole country. Switzerland has been a peaceful nation ever since. His importance as a figure of peace and brotherhood can hardly be exaggerated. Today in Switzerland, Brother Klaus is venerated by both Catholics and Protestants as the savior of their country.

REFLECTION AND DISCUSSION

1. Reflect on your own ability to forgive past failures or sins, either in yourself or in others, and to receive the grace to begin afresh. Consider an event or time when you were able to begin fresh. How might that event have ended differently had you not begun from a position of grace and courage?

2. Spend a few minutes reflecting on your own specific talents and skills. Think how these might be used in concert with others to produce greater results than you might expect if acting alone.

CHAPTER 2

Harnessing the Energies of Love for God

"The day will come when, after harnessing the ether (space), the winds, the tides and gravity, we shall harness for God the energies of love; on that day, for the second time in the history of the world, man will discover fire." (Pierre Teilhard de Chardin, *Toward the Future*, page 87)

For the past thousand years the Western world has misinterpreted love and applied the term to what the author Robert Johnson calls "romantic love" or what the Middle Ages called "courtly love." As Dr. Johnson explains in his book, *We*, we project upon an individual human being, usually one of the opposite sex, all the ideals that belong only to God and can be fulfilled only by a union with God and the accomplishment of His will.

Therefore, romantic love will always be disappointing. When the individual human being fails to live up to our projected expectations, we "fall out of love" with that person. But then our soul looks for some other human being upon which we can project our ideals of love. Once again we find ourselves "falling in love," only to be again disappointed. This explains the succession of spouses and friends which so many modern men and women choose. They are looking for an eternal, unlimited love that no human being can fulfill.

Romantic love is not true love since it is selfish love, using the beloved as an object of one's own personal pleasure and desire. True love, loving God and others the way Jesus loved, is an unselfish love which always puts the interests of God and others ahead of one's desires. True love is not easy but difficult. It requires sacrifices of one's selfish ambitions, dreams, hopes, interests. Yet it is the only form of love that brings fulfillment to us. We were created by God to love and we miss the whole purpose of our creation when we refuse to love unselfishly.

Indeed the day seems to have arrived when we can harness the energies of love for God. Because of the insights of modern depth psychology, particularly that of Carl Jung, we better understand the way love works. We now understand the habit of projecting upon other human beings the fulfillment of our love needs which only God can satisfy. We now know the psychological basis for those words of St. Augustine: "Our hearts were made for you, O God, and they shall not rest until they rest in you." The human heart or spirit is made to the image and likeness of God in the sense that it possesses some of God's infinite desires for love. No finite creature can ever fully satisfy our need for love. Carl Jung writes about the desire and hunger for the infinite God which is implanted in every human heart. This is a basic psychological need of every human being.

It still remains an open question whether we of this generation will seize this opportunity to harness for God the energies of love or by neglect forfeit it to some later generation. The decision is ours to make. It will be made as every human being, singly and then collectively, chooses to use their powers of love either to bring about God's Kingdom or to bring about one's own egocentric pleasure. When a sufficient number of individuals have understood and made the choice of love for God, the human race will enter a new age of grace, the age of Holy Spirit.

In addition to the physical, material world in which we now live, there is another world, the world of the spirit or heart where convictions are formed and decisions made. Within this interior world all that is enacted externally has its roots.

This world of the spirit is an eternal world, a sacred, holy, divine world which exists throughout the whole universe.

When a steady communication is established between the inner world of the spirit and our conscious life, we have available to us the energies of divine life and are free to harness and use them for the most good. The choice is ours. We can use or abuse these energies. Used properly we adhere to God's plan for our life and for the world and not to our plan and desires. Once we conform ourselves to God's plan, we will discover that it is infinitely more satisfying and fulfilling than any of our egocentric desires, even though this requires self-discipline and sacrifice.

Harnessing the energies of love for God is not always pleasant and easy. This can clearly be seen in the life of Jesus. It means the willingness and readiness to confront evil, wherever it is found, both in individuals and in institutions, even religious institutions. Jesus confronted the religious authorities of his day in no uncertain terms as we can see in Chapter 23 of Matthew's Gospel, and also Mark 12:38-40 and Luke 11:39-54. It was this confrontation of religious institutional evil that brought down upon Jesus the hatred and opposition of the Pharisees, the Scribes and the Sanhedrin. It eventually led to his condemnation and death on Calvary. Jesus always confronted this institutional evil in a nonviolent way but there is no doubt that it was difficult for Jesus to set himself up in opposition to the religious leaders of his day.

We need only to read Chapters 7 and 8 of John's Gospel to see how difficult it was for Jesus to harness for God the energies of love. Jesus loved his fellow countrymen very deeply and wanted so much to help them see the truth about God and their religion. Day after day he argued with them in the temple precincts, trying to convince them of the errors in their way of looking at God and the Mosaic Law. He told them, "You shall know the truth and the truth shall set you free" (John 8:32). However, their minds were imprisoned in their false attitudes towards God and the Law of Moses. In the end, Jesus had to die for his convictions. He failed to convince most of his listeners. This is often the price we need to pay in order to harness for God the energies of love.

By possessing the power to love we share to some extent in the infinite power of God Himself. By sharing with us the power to love, God has limited to some extent His own infinite power. He must wait upon us to decide how we will use the gift of human freedom: whether we will use it to love God and others unconditionally and selflessly or whether we will use it to do evil. To harness for God the energies of love means always to use the energy of love in a positive way to help others and to further God's plans for the Kingdom of love upon earth.

Love gives us a share in the very life and energy of God Himself. St. John says that God is love (I John 4:8). Therefore, to the extent we practice an unconditional love similar to the way God loves, we share in the infinite power and energy of God. This is an awesome responsibility. As far as we know no other creature on earth shares in this divine power and energy of love. Animal mothers show a loving care for their offspring but this is not freely given but is under the compulsion of animal instinct.

Unconditional Love

When we harness for God the energies of love we endeavor to love with the same unconditional love which God practices. Unconditional love is present when we consistently put the needs of God and others ahead of our desires. Notice, this does not say that we should put the desires of the beloved ahead of our desires, but only the needs of the beloved. Each time we love unconditionally we have to make a reasonable judgment whether it is a legitimate need the other person has. If so, then it must be placed ahead of our desires.

A problem arises when it is a choice between the legitimate needs of the beloved and our own legitimate needs. A decision must be made regarding which need is the greatest and the most important. It is often possible that a personal need will have to take precedence over a lesser need of the beloved. If the needs of both are somewhat equal, unconditional love would expect us to sacrifice our need for the sake of the beloved. We have the example of Father Kolbe, who sacrificed his own life in the Nazi death camp in order to save the life of a fellow prisoner.

We have an example of unconditional love in the love which God has for each of us. God desires very much to establish His Kingdom of justice and mercy in this present time. However, S/He is willing to put our need of human freedom ahead of His desire for the Kingdom. This explains why the Kingdom has been delayed for so long. It is clear from the Christian Gospels that God wanted to establish the divine Kingdom on earth 2000 years ago when Jesus walked this earth. However, this Kingdom of God's love could not be established without our free cooperation. Out of respect for human freedom, God has delayed His Kingdom all these centuries.

We are commanded to show unconditional love for God. This is the meaning of the first great commandment to love God with all our heart, all our soul, all our mind and all our strength. This is how Jesus taught his disciples to live. In the Lord's Prayer Jesus gives us the perfect model to follow in our prayer and in the way we live. The first half of the Lord's Prayer is concerned with God's needs. We only address our needs in the second half of the prayer. If we love God unconditionally, our first concern will always be to discern and pray for God's needs. Only then should we ask God's help in caring for our needs.

Not only should we put God's needs ahead of our desires, we are commanded by Jesus to love others the way he loved his disciples. That means we should consistently put the needs of others ahead of our desires. These others include the whole human race and not just our immediate family and friends. In order to practice unconditional love for others we need to study closely the Gospel accounts of how Jesus loved his disciples, for example, Peter and John, the beloved disciple. Jesus loved them in accord with God's will and plan. Jesus loved them enough to die for them. Jesus was always ready to forgive them even when they abandoned him and denied that they knew him. Some weeks later over another charcoal fire by the Lake of Galilee Jesus asks Peter three times to profess his love for him. By means of unconditional love, Jesus then entrusts to Peter the care of Christ's flock.

REFLECTION AND DISCUSSION

1. Select someone you see as a heroine or hero in the spiritual dimension. List ways in which that person has lived unconditional love and the consequences of the energetic commitment of that person to love as God loves.

2. Where do you see opportunities in your own life to mirror the same kind of commitment?

CHAPTER 3

The Nature of Love

Knowledge, Revelation, Benevolence,
Union, God-Centeredness

Love can be experienced in an infinite variety of ways. We may experience spousal love, filial love, parental love, agapic love, erotic love, and sexual love. Every experience of love is different. Nevertheless, five distinct elements can be discerned in each authentic encounter of love between two persons, whether between God and oneself or another human being and oneself. We first become aware of love when we find ourselves desiring to know all we can about that person. This is followed by a willingness to reveal all about ourselves to the beloved. A third element is the effort to do all we can to please the other, whether God or a human being. Fourth, all lovers want to be in close proximity to each other. Finally, every true love relationship must be centered in God or those transcendental qualities which describe God's essential nature. These are truth, justice, goodness, unity and beauty. When these five dispositions are present in both parties to the relationship, we have the fulfillment of love so desired by everyone.

The first delight experienced by a lover is the fascination one feels for the least detail of the other's character and life. Everything one sees in the other strikes a responsive chord within one's being. Having discovered this new world of the beloved which one had never previously suspected to exist, one's great interest in life is to study the object of love. The more one learns, the more attracted one becomes to the other person. Never was the process of learning so enjoyable as when it is a study of the beloved. Most wonderful of all, the other person seems to possess an inexhaustible store of beauty, truth and goodness.

A lover is not satisfied merely to know all one can about the object of love. In the second stage of love there is a desire to reveal to the other person everything about oneself. What a joy it is for both to discover how much they have in common—the same secret dreams and desires which they had imagined no one else possessed but themselves. What a delightful surprise it is to find someone with whom one is able to share the most intimate thoughts and hopes. Never again will one be absolutely alone. There will always be at least one person with whom everything can be shared.

Another desire that manifests itself is benevolence towards the beloved. During this third stage of love, one wants to do everything possible to make the other person happy. One wants the beloved to be the most perfect, the most beautiful, the happiest person possible; and one will do all in one's power to see that this is accomplished. One will go to any extreme to show love and is willing to dedicate one's life to the other, whether that person be God or another human being.

The goal of all true love is permanent union with the beloved, but this union is possible only if the other person also desires it. Both parties must freely choose to give themselves in love to each other; otherwise no real union can be attained. Nevertheless, in the fourth stage of love, the lover will do all in his/her power to encourage the other to say "Yes" to the proposal of love. If the love is great, one will literally beg for a return of love, exposing one's whole soul to the possibility of being deeply hurt if the offer is spurned. Union with the beloved becomes the "pearl of great price" that makes no sacrifice too great to make.

The fifth element of love is one frequently overlooked by human beings seeking to establish an authentic encounter of love. Every love affair must be centered in God and in accord with God's plan for creation. Otherwise, it will be disappointing and a failure. Every human heart craves for a union with God. No human being is fully satisfied until possessing God and living in accord with God's plan of creation. When we seek to satisfy our longing for love apart from God and God's plan, we will always be disappointed. This is why romantic love never fully satisfies a person. If, however, there is a mutual love between two human beings that is fully in accord with God's will, this will be truly satisfying and fulfilling.

Authentic love may be present in the life of a professed atheist, provided the atheist subscribes to the all-importance of those essential qualities of God which we call transcendental values. These qualities are truth, justice, goodness, beauty and unity. Since these comprise the essence of God, anyone who believes in them is actually believing in God, but by another name. Almost without exception atheists are atheists because they reject the image of God which believers in God profess to follow.

Difficulties in Human Love

Since one can never be sure what response another human being will make to our proposal of love, it is easy to see the possibility of great pain when we open ourselves to love. Because of the possibility that the offer of love will be spurned, many people are afraid to love. However, having once tasted the wonderful joy of being in love, one will usually be willing to pay the high price required of a lover. This is why it is so important to give others, especially the young, as many experiences of unselfish love as possible. If they have had a number of satisfying situations of being loved and cherished, they will then be more ready to open their own hearts toward others. Love or lack of love in childhood and youth will greatly influence the ability to love and be loved in adult life.

Love would be difficult enough if we had to contend only with ourselves, but both parties must freely accept and follow all five of the desires necessary to the fullness of love. In the first glow of attraction everything may seem easily attained, but actually a lifetime of effort is required to bring love to an optimum completion. This is true not only of marriage but of every worthwhile friendship, including that between God and ourselves. In the present condition of life, suffering in some form will always be connected with love. Even our Lord and the Blessed Mother were unable to love without passing through the crucible of pain. The greater the worth of the love, the greater the price to pay. During the growth of love toward union a number of crises usually develop of which the outcome is uncertain. Either there will be doubts about our own ability to measure up to the demands of love, or we await the decision of the other party to make a return of love.

It is possible for a crisis to develop at any step along the path to love. We may be greatly fascinated at first, but as we come to know the other person more intimately, we may find many things that we do not like. The beloved may also discover qualities in us that are not pleasing. With each of these revelations a decision has to be made to continue or terminate the relationship. A mature individual will weigh both sides and make a free decision in the best interests of both parties.

In the process of opening ourselves to the beloved, other crises arise. There may be secrets of our past life which we hesitate to reveal. We are torn between the desire to be completely open with the other and the fear that the relationship will end if the beloved knows us as really we are. The more insecure we are, the more fearful we will be of losing the other's love. Those who have a particularly low opinion of themselves and lack self-confidence, will go through intense suffering when they expose the secret depths of their souls to the beloved.

In the beginning there seems to be nothing we would refuse to do to make the beloved happy. Sooner or later, however, there will be clashes between our own selfish interests and service to the other's needs. In the intimacy of love it is not possible to conceal our basic selfishness from the eyes of the beloved. We may grow tired or lazy and find the constant effort to please the other person too much trouble. If the beloved is also selfish, it becomes even more difficult for us to keep putting out the effort needed to serve him/her. We will see how the other takes advantage of our love at times and demands an unreasonable service of us. In these conflicts of interest, decisions must be made; and sometimes it will be judged best to terminate the relationship. At other times, the value of the love is so great that one decides to increase one's generosity and benevolence toward the other instead of breaking the relationship.

Many different degrees of union are possible with the beloved. Real union is achieved only with another person, not with an animal or a thing. Therefore we must be able to see the beloved as a person and not as a thing or mere object. The more areas in which both can find compatibility, the easier it will be to attain unity. Agreement should exist at least on the ultimate questions of life. Both should have more or less the same depth of emotional life as well as the same level of intellectual and cultural values. The more mature both are, the closer the union.

Finally, it is not at all easy to keep human love God-centered. God's plans for us frequently clash with our plans, our desires, hopes, dreams. It takes much self-discipline to sacrifice our human desires of love when they are not in accord with God's will. The sacrifice of human love for the sake of God will occur only if our love of God is greater than our love for human beings. Otherwise, we will seek in vain to satisfy our desires of love apart from God's plans for us.

Because of sin, our ability to love has been seriously weakened. Ordinarily we are capable of having only a few close friendships in life, and even these need special help from God in order to develop and to persevere. The greater one's capacity for love, the higher the price that must be paid to fulfill this potential.

Unless one has been thoroughly trained in self-control and generosity, there is grave danger that one will refuse to make the sacrifices necessary for the union of love. In time of crisis, instead of progressing forward into greater maturity, one may choose to regress. At the moment, one may imagine that the lower level of existence offers greater attractions than the higher but more difficult level of unity with the beloved. But as time goes on, if the lover declines the challenges of the love relationship, life often becomes more and more frustrating. In the frustration and dissatisfaction of remaining in the lower level of unity, God is calling one to return to the tasks of love. In this way, one progresses into deeper unity with the lover.

If this call of grace is obeyed, earlier losses can often be regained, provided one is willing to pay the extra price of suffering and effort. Anyone who has tasted the joy of love will not have to be convinced of the value of friendship. The problem exists for those who for one reason or another have never had a true experience of love. Words have never been capable of adequately describing the beauties of love. The only way to help a person who does not appreciate love is to give him/her one's own unselfish love. The older a person is and the more one has been hurt in the past by the lack of love, the more difficult it is to penetrate the hard shell that has grown around the heart. Yet, love is so exceedingly good that we should go to any extreme to help others experience this most wonderful of powers that God has shared with us.

If we have been recipients of a true and unselfish love from others, we have a duty to share it with those who have not been so blessed. We should go out in friendship to every neglected soul and every hardened heart. Their inability to love may be due to an excessive fear of God, themselves and others. They may lack the necessary inner security that is needed to bestow their love on others. They may be afraid of having their love rejected. Convinced that others are out to get them, they find it difficult to trust anyone. They may imagine that they will offend God if they allow themselves to love human beings. Regardless of the cause, they need help and it is our duty to go out to them in love.

REFLECTION AND DISCUSSION

1. Consider a significant love relationship in your life. How does that relationship reflect each of these five elements? Which element requires you to be most diligent in effort?

2. As a spiritual community, we have an obligation to express God's love, particularly toward those who are marginalized, alienated, or difficult to love. When have you been difficult to love, and who loved you through that stage?

CHAPTER 4

The Objects of Our Love

There are many kinds of love, depending upon the particular object which we love. Strictly speaking, it is possible only to love another person, whether that person be God or another human being. Yet, in our ordinary human speech we speak of loving money, loving ourselves, loving the world. "Loving" an inanimate object is of an entirely different nature from the union of love with another person. It is possible to use "love" in this loose sense as long as we are clear that our feeling is not love, but desire on our part to be united with or more possibly, to possess that object. As long as we keep this distinction in mind, we can speak of loving ourselves or loving the world.

In general, the objects of love fall under four headings: God, our neighbor, the world and ourselves. The beginning of all love is respect for the one to be loved. Persons and things are to be treated with reverence for their nature and purpose and not in accord with our own selfish desires and needs. Reverence is especially necessary in our relationship with God. Our love for God must always bear in mind the infinite distance that separates us from our Creator, but fear of God should never dominate our prayers and other actions toward God. God has called us to love Him/Her with our whole heart, with our whole soul, with our whole strength and with our whole mind (Lk 10:27). This first and greatest commandment of God should leave no doubt in our minds about the all-importance of love in our relationship with God. It is the greatest of all possible loves that we can experience in this present life or in a future life. All other loves are a training ground to prepare us for this supreme love of God.

Experiences of human love should make it easier for us to love God. There are three general forms of human love: parental, friendly and spousal. Each of these is different, yet all of them should contain the five elements explained in the previous chapter. If both parties to the love freely choose to make the necessary effort to develop all five of these desires or dispositions, then they will experience true love, that most wonderful of all God's gifts. To reach maturity, the normal person needs to know something about all three loves: love of parents, love of friends, love of a spouse. At one time or another in our life we need to have been loved by parents or by someone who took the place of parents; by someone whom we can call a friend; by someone we can consider a spouse, either physically or spiritually. To attain wholeness in our own life, we need to have given ourselves in love to others; first as a child to a parent and later as a parent to children, whether they be physical children or spiritual children; second, as a friend to other friends; third, either physically or spiritually as a spouse to another spouse. The more experience we have of love, the more mature we will become.

God has given us these three forms of human love in order to help us understand and appreciate the three ways God loves us. God loves us as a parent, as a friend, as a spouse. These three aspects of God's love form the three persons of the Blessed Trinity. Therefore a true love and devotion for the Divine Trinity will express itself in our three-fold love of God. We love God as the obedient child of a divine Father/Mother. We love God as our brother/sister or friend. We love God with a spousal love.

There is a necessary order and balance among the many different persons we are called to love. Since both our time and energy are limited, we must make our decisions of love according to the particular needs of those involved. Mistakes will often be made in our decisions of love, but if we are sincere, God will guide us on the right path. The important thing in life is that we never stop loving others as best we can. Jesus in the Gospel tells us, "This is my commandment, love one another as I have loved you. There is no greater love than this, to lay down one's life for one's friends" (Jn 15:12-13). And how did Jesus love his disciples? He loved them by consistently putting their interests ahead of his own. This then is the love to which all Christians are called.

Besides the love we should give to God and our neighbor, there are two other forms of love that are necessary: a proper love of the world and a proper love of ourselves. The danger of going to excess in our love for the world and ourselves is considerably greater than when we are loving God and our fellow human beings. For one thing, it is beneath our human dignity to seek the same intimate union with things of the world or with our own ego that we should desire with God and other persons. A union of love implies equality and it is never right to put ourselves on an equal level with an animal, money, property, pleasure, or our ego. It is even worse when we allow these lower creatures to enslave us so that they become our masters and we their servants.

Probably the greatest of all dangers lies in our becoming enslaved to our ego. The ego is the center of our conscious life; the real center of our nature is the inner self or the person which is hidden in the depths of our inner being. Sacred Scripture commands us to love this inner "self" and gives it as the standard for our love of our neighbor. "You shall love your neighbor as you love your *self*" (Lk 10:27). Problems arise when we substitute the ego as the center of our lives. This easily degenerates into a worship of our ego which we call self-idolatry. In like manner when we speak of selfishness we really mean egotism.

According to Carl Jung, the fundamental task in attaining maturity is to establish the authenticity of the ego. This means that it must be trained to know and keep its proper place as the servant of our inner being, which in turn should be subject to God and God's laws. When our inner self rebels against God, our ego in turn rebels against our own inner self. Instead of remaining a servant to the self, the ego seeks to become the ruler and master of our whole life. Authenticity is established when the ego is brought under control and taught to be a good servant in the service of the real ruler: our inner self. This inner self in turn must be under obedience to the Holy Spirit who dwells in the depth of every human being. If the ego will work hard to perform its appointed tasks, it will succeed in subjecting all the powers and faculties of our human nature to our inner person and this inner person, in turn, shall be put at the service of God.

One of the tests of a well-centered and authentic person is the absence of anxiety and insecurity in regard to oneself. Instead of fear, our attitude will be one of love, a proper, well-ordered and real love for ourselves. Unless we have a proper respect for ourselves, we will never be able to enter into a proper relationship of love with God and neighbor. Authenticity of the ego, therefore, is the foundation for growth in wholeness, both naturally and supernaturally. It is impossible for the egocentric person to be either a saint or a naturally mature person. The reason is that an egotist does not know how to love or chooses to love the wrong things and in the wrong way.

The tasks of love are without a doubt the most important of all the work given us to accomplish upon earth. The success of everything, both of nature and grace, depends upon the happy solution of the many problems involved in our learning to love. We cannot expect an easy or quick attainment of perfection in this art. It requires a lifetime of struggle amid many conflicts and failures. The greater our potential for love, the more difficult it will be to control it. This, however, does not mean that we need to be struggling continuously. There is a time for the enjoyment of peace and the other wonderful fruits of love. The more proficiency we have attained in our ability to love, the greater and more frequent will be our periods of joy and happiness with our friends. Even for those who must work hard to develop their extraordinary potential for love, there is need for periods of quiet enjoyment of their love. On the other hand, if we find ourselves going through life without any real struggles or conflicts with egocentricity or other abuses of love, this is nearly always an indication that we have stopped increasing our capacity for love and have settled for a life of mediocrity.

One area of struggle is the conflict between our duties to life on this earth and our responsibility to use our present life to prepare for life after death. Many people try to resolve this constant tension by denying the value of one or the other. Those who choose to give all their effort to this present earthly life, either deny the existence of life after death or simply ignore it. Sometimes those who opt for life after death neglect to give sufficient attention to their responsibilities to this present earthly life. The more mature and holy we become, the less conflict we will experience between these two areas of our life.

Any sort of dualism between nature and grace is contrary to the revelation of Christ which insists that nature not be destroyed but be incarnated and lifted up to a divine level. Grace should build on nature and the more sound and healthy is our whole nature of body and spirit, the less difficult it will be to attain sanctity. As far as possible, growth in natural maturity should keep pace with growth in sanctity. We must struggle to attain this constant balance and tension between the two, but it is a consolation to know that the more we grow in wholeness, the less difficult the effort usually becomes. What a joy it is to discover that ultimately and basically there is no actual conflict between these two forms of love, nature and grace. They are the two sides of the gift of God's creation. For the sake of a better appreciation of God's gifts, we make a distinction between our God-given nature and all those special, supernatural gifts of grace generously bestowed on us out of the pure goodness of God's heart.

REFLECTION AND DISCUSSION

1. Select one area in which you are having trouble expressing your love (God, neighbor, world, self) Write a dialogue with the Holy Spirit about your difficulty. Write both parts of the conversation. You speak first and then wait for the Holy Spirit to respond. In turn, you reply or question further. Set the written conversation aside for review later during the day or week. If you wish, continue the written conversation at that time, asking for discernment and support in expressing your love.

2. How is the ability to love others related to a proper love of self?

CHAPTER 5

Natural Love of God

The ultimate goal of all love is the love of God. Other forms of love have value in themselves; nevertheless they would never have existed except through creation by God's love. If we use these created loves properly, they will lead us toward the love of God and never away from it. Among the created loves which God has seen fit to share with us, we can distinguish two fundamental categories. All those natural forms of love about which we spoke in the last chapter are included in the first category. The second category is the higher and more important one: the supernatural love which we call grace-life.

One might imagine that a study of nature would yield unquestioning proof of God's love for us. If we had not sinned, this would have been the case. However, because of sin we imagine that God is actually hostile to our best interests, keeping us from becoming like God. We find it hard to see the loving hand of God behind the many outward appearances of evil. We often call something evil that is merely difficult to attain. Throughout history the human race has made the same mistake that is symbolically described in the first chapters of Genesis. We consider the will of God for us as hostile because God is unwilling to give us the reward of love without strenuous efforts on our part. This hostility to God in our human experience is called by St. Paul the *sarx.* Unfortunately this is usually translated as the *flesh* (Gal 5:17). Thus, a prejudice against the body and everything of flesh has arisen in our Christian tradition. We will explore this problem more fully in Chapter 8.

In our laziness we would like for love to be easily attained. Actually love is the fruit of labor and those unwilling to work for it do not receive the fruits of love. At first sight, it may seem that the greater good for us would be to have a life of unending ease and comfort. In reality, this is contrary to our nature as well as God's nature. "My Father works until now and I work" (Jn 5:17). When God created the human race we were commanded to dress and keep the garden. Now that we live under the curse of human sin, the effort necessary to attain love is even greater. "Cursed be the ground because of you; in toil shall you eat of it all the days of your life; thorns and thistles shall it bring forth to you ... In the sweat of your brow shall you eat bread" (Gn 3:17-19).

When a child is suffering from the chastisement of an angry father, it is quite difficult to realize that the hand which punishes is a loving hand. Yet common sense tells us that this can be true. Therefore when we study nature today, it is possible to see the love of God even in the thorns and thistles that now form our correction. "The discipline of the Lord disdain not; spurn not his reproof, for whom the Lord loves, he reproves and he chastises the son he favors" (Prv 3:11-12). Granting the fact of sin in the world, we should realize the need of discipline and hard work in order to attain the love that is our goal.

Contaminated as we are by the blindness of sin, it is rather easy for us to conjure up the picture of a hostile God, lacking in genuine love for us. Without special help from God we would never be able to see through the appearances of evil in nature and discern the loving hand of a heavenly parent behind them. But even with the grace of faith, much effort is often required to see God's love in the world of nature and to make a return of love to God. This uncertainty of all natural love serves a very useful purpose in bringing out our real character. Anyone can love when it is easy. True love is proven best in times of crisis. In difficulties we may be tempted to think that God does not really love us. God appears to be anything but a benevolent, loving parent. We search for God and S/He seems to have withdrawn from us. We look for the five elements of love in God's dealings with us and we imagine that none of them can be found. For a time our whole relationship with God hangs in the balance. It is then that we are challenged to make a decision either for or against God.

It is during these critical moments of life that nature needs help from the outside. If the crisis is not too great, another human being may be able to restore our faith and trust in a loving God. Frequently only God's grace can redeem us from the depth of despair which we may feel towards God. But grace alone is not enough. There must be a willingness on our part to accept that grace and cooperate with it. In Sacred Scripture God has promised to be faithful to us and give us the necessary aid to overcome our natural despair (I Cor 10:13). God promises to enlighten our minds to know and see the truth of God's love (Phil 2:13). We have God's assurance that grace will strengthen our wills to make the effort necessary to believe, to trust and to love. But never will the Divine Lover force us against our wills to make a decision to love. If we use our freedom to decide against God, it will never be because we lacked the needed light and strength from God to accept the grace to love. We may blame Satan and evil companions for influencing us, but ultimately, the responsibility rests squarely upon our own shoulders.

It is a difficult task to have an encounter of love with anyone. When this person is God, the effort required is often great. Some people have the idea that loving God is easy. We little realize that if God should appear before us in all the tremendous divine power, we would be so over-awed that we would only want to flee from God's sight. "My face you cannot see for no one sees me and still lives" (Ex 33:20). Even the voice of God makes us tremble with fear. "On hearing (the voice) the disciples fell on their faces and were exceedingly afraid" (Mt 17:6). God is quite different from the idea most of us have of Him/Her.

Without a deep conversion of our natural knowledge of God, it is impossible to have a true union of love with God. We must allow our nature to be transformed until it is capable of meeting God on a divine level. Natural effort cannot do this. God's help is necessary for transcendence to take place. Frequently our nature rebels against such an incarnation. We do not want to abandon the habitat of nature because it seems at first sight that the supernatural will destroy the natural. If we imagine that the love of God requires the loss of our nature, we will resist such a change with all the powers of our natural being. We do not want to open ourselves in love to a God who will require us to abandon all that we have come to cherish in our nature. For example, we love our human freedom and the power it gives us to do as we choose. So we resist when even our own common sense tells us that God would be more pleased if we acted otherwise. We imagine that God does not have our best interests at heart.

Many crises will develop in our attempts to attain a union of love with God. Again and again we may question the value of the five elements necessary for a sincere love of God. We are not so sure that we want to know all about this God who at times seems so demanding. We hesitate to open ourselves to a God in whom we find it difficult to have complete confidence. We have no feelings of benevolence toward one who appears so often to be anything but benevolent towards us. We have no desire for any union of love with a God who seems so contradictory in many ways. We fail at the final element of love, that of dwelling mutually with God in the God-like qualities of truth, justice, goodness, unity, and beauty. If left to our natural efforts, we would often have a distorted picture of God who would be impossible to love. As St. Thomas Aquinas states, "The truth concerning God, investigated by natural reason, will be attained by very few persons, only after a long time and even then with an admixture of errors" (Summa Theologica, Pars Prima, Q.1, A.1).

The history of the human race is living proof of the value of a knowledge and love of God. Depth psychologists have proved in a scientific way that there is a natural capacity in human nature to know and love God. Just as we have the five bodily senses to make contact with physical reality, so God has implanted certain spiritual organs or functions in our psyche to make contact with

God and spiritual realities. They enable us to make contact with the psychic, spiritual world and, if properly developed, they enable us to enter into a natural relationship of love with God. It is the task of all religions to develop these natural, religious capacities in our nature. If these religious archetypes or organs are left undeveloped, all kinds of neurotic conflicts result, especially during the second half of life on earth. Therefore, even from the point of natural maturity, it is necessary that we establish a proper relationship with God. Not only does the mature person need a love-relationship with oneself, with the world and with other human beings, we cannot attain the wholeness of our nature without a loving relationship with a personal God who is creator and supreme Lord of all creation.

Intuitively realizing their need for God, nearly all human beings have sought this relationship through the practice of some sort of religion. Unfortunately one of the effects of sin is that our intellect is darkened and our whole personality weakened. Therefore, so often natural religion becomes seriously distorted in theory and practice. However, God has not abandoned us to our ignorance and weakness. God has come to our aid throughout the history of the human race. These divine revelations were never forced upon us but merely offered. At times we have accepted God's special help and benefited greatly from it. Often we have rejected the offer of grace and enlightenment and attempted to set up some form of natural religion. Before the coming of Jesus, when divine revelation was limited to a small group of people, these natural religions elicited the best that might be expected from the human race. With the advent of Christ and the worldwide proclamation of the

Christian gospel, these natural religions are no longer sufficient. Frequently they have become the enemies of Christianity. On the other hand, the great, non-Christian religions such as Jewish, Muslim, Buddhist and Hindu religions contain much that is true and good. The hope is that Christians as well as non-Christians will be open to the truths of each other and thus bring about a unity of true faith in God.

In our present Western civilization, natural forms of religion are practiced in a variety of ways. There are, for example, those who make a religion of service to their fellow human beings. They consider the hidden God too far away to be taken seriously. The many, great needs of suffering humanity are more immediate, so they become great humanitarians and social workers. If they are wealthy, they become philanthropists, handsomely endowing different foundations for the betterment of the human race. Often they are sincerely motivated by a genuine love for their fellow human beings, but Jesus Christ and the Christian faith may be completely absent from their life. Though they may be considered religious, it is a natural form of religion called secular humanism.

Others may have some knowledge of God and Christ, but be unwilling to make any commitment to a particular form of religion, remaining outside all organized religious bodies in proud isolation and tolerating the existence of churches only for weak creatures who need these props. For themselves, they are content to stand alone in their man-made relationship with the God of their choice. Because they make their own religious rules, there will seldom be any conflict between what they want and what they think God is asking of them.

A third form of natural religion exists today in the worship of psychology. Because of the tremendous discoveries in this field of psychology during the present century, the cult of psychology is a particularly dangerous form of natural religion. In no way does this justify our ignoring the new insights into human nature, which the psychologists have discovered in recent generations. Because of the danger of going astray into a false form of religion, it is all the more necessary for Christians to understand psychology and to help those in this field to see its Christian implications. Otherwise we may well awaken a generation from now to face an anti-Christian psychology that would be militantly religious in its efforts to destroy all other forms of religion, including the Christian church.

There is another form of natural religion that is found among those who are members of Christian churches and who consider themselves practicing Christians. These are the individualists who feel no special commitment towards the Christian community but only personally to God. There is, of course, the need of balance between individual and community and it is possible to go to extremes in either direction. However, our greatest problem at present is awakening individual Christians to the needs of the community and the world.

Since liturgy is a group experience, there can be no progress in liturgical worship as long as the majority of the congregation insist on worshiping God in their own little, private, individualistic way. Because of the lack of good, authentic liturgical experiences, many Christians have had only individual encounters with God, coming to know and love God privately, apart from the community. They have developed their own individual form of prayer-life and worship, even when attending a public liturgy with the community. The more satisfaction they have found in these personal encounters with Christ, the more they now resent the distractions of joining in a community form of worship. They feel that they cannot pray or make contact with their God when everyone around them is singing or praying aloud. They think of the church as a quiet place, conducive to deep meditation on the things of God. They feel no obligation towards joining with others to attain a communal encounter with God, since this is a religious experience of which they are ignorant. It comes as quite a shock to these people to be told that it is contrary to the Christian religion to insist upon the private character of liturgical worship.

It is necessary that all natural love of God be united with supernatural grace. Unless these natural religious experiences are incarnated and elevated to the supernatural level, they soon become enemies of God instead of friends. Once we grant the fact that God has called us to a special union of love with the Blessed Trinity, all natural forms of religion become insufficient. They may serve as teachers who prepare us for Christ, but they become enemies of Christianity if they insist on being the highest way of loving God. Depth psychology and the various forms of modern, natural religion can do a great service to Christianity by helping us to discover and develop our natural capacity for God. There is a vast portion of the human race in which the natural religious archetypes are still asleep—untamed, uncultivated, untapped. As long as this remains true, these persons cannot even attain natural maturity, let alone the supernatural encounters of divine grace. However, there is a danger that in awakening these archetypes of natural religion, they will be used merely as a means towards the development of natural maturity and not for the supernatural encounter with God by grace.

Once our natural capacity for God is awakened, many conflicts will arise between God's interests and what seems to be self-interest. In order to convert our natural love for God into a supernatural love, help from God is needed as well as many sacrifices of our own selfish desires. Any basic change in our nature requires effort and struggle on our part. But once converted, a wonderful change takes place in our whole being. This awakening of supernatural faith and love for God is immensely greater than the experience of falling in love with another human being. Every faculty of our being is aroused and intensified. For the first time, we become aware of our true significance before God. All of our other powers for love are increased so that immense progress is made in the wholeness of nature as well as grace. We now have a true presentiment of what life is really meant to be. Our personality awakens in all its fullness. Through the quiet voice of our conscience, our divine lover reveals to us most intimate secrets and desires. Each time we open our hearts in love and correspond with God's call of grace, our whole life takes another giant step forward toward wholeness.

REFLECTION AND DISCUSSION

1. Consider a time in which you experienced a crisis that made it difficult to love. How was or is that event being resolved? How have you become more mature in your ability to love God, yourself, and others because of the crisis?

2. It is in the nature of human beings to seek a spiritual aspect; that is, mankind in general experiences a need for "natural religion." What aspects of a "natural religion" have been divinized in your spiritual journey and to what effect on your journey of faith?

CHAPTER 6

The Abuse of Love

Pharisaism

In our relationship with God, probably the most frequent abuse of love is to treat God as a thing rather than a person. This was the sin of the Pharisees which our Lord condemned so often and so strongly. Instead of making religion a personal relationship of love, the Pharisees made it a business deal: I will give God these things, if he will give me eternal salvation. No matter how much we give God, S/He is not satisfied unless we give Her/Him ourselves in wholehearted love. Religion is not a question of the quantity of external actions and things that we offer to God. Rather it is the quality and intensity of the commitment of love that we are willing to make to Her/Him. The Pharisee was unwilling to make this surrender of his whole person in love to God. He tried to satisfy his religious obligations by a scrupulous adherence to the external laws of God. He occupied himself with the accidental details and formalities of worship, while neglecting the inner spirit of a devoted love. The personal relationship of Jesus to God was a constant witness against the absence of love in the religion of the Pharisees. Unwilling to rid themselves of their Pharisaism, they turned in hatred upon Jesus and killed him.

Throughout the centuries of Christianity, the evil of Pharisaism has continued to haunt the lives of Christians who are unwilling or unable to love God in a personal way. It is so much easier to dispose of our religious obligations when it is a matter of fulfilling the mere letter of the law. To love a person is a very difficult and demanding task. When this person is an invisible God, the task of loving becomes even more difficult. Thanks to God's constant helping grace and thanks to the coming of God to earth in human flesh, the task of having a personal love for God is both possible and tremendously satisfying. The first step to attain a proper relationship of love with God is to become aware of how much the spirit of the Pharisees has pervaded our own religious practices. Are we excessively preoccupied with the number and quantity of our prayers, with rubrics and other accidentals of worship? Is our attitude the juridical attitude of the Pharisees or the pastoral attitude of Jesus? Are we more concerned with laws or with persons? Are we too literal in stressing conformity to the letter of the law to the neglect of a personal love for God? If we love God as we should, we will find a place for all these things, but never will we allow them to take precedence over the task of attaining a personal love for God.

Pride and Conceit

At the origin of the Pharisees' problem was pride. St. Thomas Aquinas says that pride is the beginning of all abuses of love. He defines pride as the exaggerated love of one's own excellence to the contempt of God. The greatest contempt we can show God is to treat God as a thing rather than a person. This frequently occurs when we are wrapped up in ourselves and our own interests and have no time to be concerned about anyone else, God included. We treat everyone, even God, as something to be used for our own advantage or amusement. The only person we take seriously is ourself and, in due time, this leads to self-idolatry. Pride is an exaggeration of the proper estimate we should have of the good which God has bestowed on us. The first step to overcome pride is to thank God for all the goodness we see in ourselves as well as others, giving the credit for all this good to God. The next step is to identify the many devious forms that pride and conceit take in our life. How do we treat others, both God and neighbor? Do we strive to let our hearts go out to them in love and loving service or do we treat them as things and use them for our own benefit? Remembering how Jesus identified himself with all our brothers and sisters, we will realize that any contempt we show for other human beings is likewise showing contempt for God and therefore is the sin of pride and conceit.

Vanity

Not only do we abuse love by showing contempt for our neighbors, we are also guilty of abuse when we exaggerate the importance of the good opinion of our neighbors. This is called vanity, which is an excessive desire for the approval of others. Lacking a sense of inner security, the vain person becomes a slave to human respect. He will go to almost any extreme to obtain praise and honor from others. The desire to please one's fellow human beings becomes more important than the desire to please God. A vain person makes all his judgments in the light of what other people will think, especially those people upon whom he depends in one way or another. Lacking confidence in ourselves, we become slaves to public opinion. Because vanity is such a childish fault, most adults are unwilling to face up to the extent that it motivates their actions. The ability to conceal it usually succeeds only in the eyes of the vain person. Most other people see rather quickly through the more or less crude attempts that are made to obtain praise, honor and the good opinion of others. If anyone wishes to be cured of this fault, one should start with the assumption that one has some vanity of which one is now unaware. The next step is to find an honest friend who will remind us of this fault of vanity each time it appears. After that it may require a lifetime of effort to bring about the proper balance in our love and respect for the desires of others. Through faith and hope in God we can gain that self-confidence and inner security that will enable us to be properly independent of the opinions of others.

Covetousness

The lack of inner peace and security shows itself in other ways besides vanity. St. Thomas Aquinas claims (in *Summa Theologica*) that covetousness is the root of all sins. He defines covetousness as the exaggerated love of created things. A modern term for covetousness is addiction. The covetous person has such an overwhelming desire for the things of this world that he will go to any extreme to obtain them. The covetous person is not satisfied with what he now possesses. He allows himself to become obsessively attracted to the temporal goods of money, property, food, drink, pleasure, etc. We turn from the proper love of God only when we allow ourselves to be captivated by an excessive love for some creature of God. The more insecure we are in our possession of God, the more we feel the need of money, property, food and other temporal goods. If we surrender to these desires, gradually, imperceptibly we become enslaved to one or more of them: food, drink, tobacco, coffee, sex, clothes, nice car, beautiful home, fine furniture, brilliant conversation, bridge club, antiques, expensive vacation, travel, bank account, large property holdings, power, high office or any of a host of other creature comforts.

There is a place for all of these worldly things, provided we put the things of God first. The danger of covetousness is that we give lip service to God, while actually making a false god of one or more of God's creatures. The first step to overcome this slavery to the things of this world is to recognize how greatly we are attracted to the goods of this world. Because we have grossly exaggerated their value, we feel very insecure when deprived of them. To overcome this insecurity we must take time to build up a great confidence in God. As we grow in the knowledge and trust and love of God, our fears and anxiety about the goods of this world will lessen. If we can experience some real encounters of love with God, the attractiveness of the world will proportionately lessen.

Avarice/Greed

Of all the forms of covetousness, both the Bible (I Tim 6:10) and Thomas Aquinas insist that avarice or greed is the most difficult one to overcome. Avarice is the exaggerated love of money and material goods. The more insecure one feels within oneself, the more one will feel the need of amassing a large quantity of wealth. Therefore, once we have faced up to the presence of greed within our souls, the next step is to try to counteract it by increasing our confidence in God. Through the love that is given and received from God, we will begin to experience a legitimate self-confidence that will enable us to break the chains of greed that enslave our souls. The more peace and inner security we feel with God, the less fear we will have of being without the necessary goods of this world.

Gluttony

Another form of covetousness is gluttony, which is the excessive desire for the pleasures of food and drink. This is particularly difficult to master because we must learn the habit of moderation, especially in the matter of food. Human nature is so constructed that it is easier to give up something entirely than it is to use it with moderation. Yet moderation is essential in almost everything in life. Therefore, the self-control that we are able to develop in eating will enable us to practice the virtue of temperance elsewhere. For this reason, Jesus places fasting almost on an equal footing with prayer as a means to rid ourselves of evil. "This kind of evil spirit can be cast out in no way except by prayer and fasting" (Mt 17:21). Without many experiences of fasting it is often impossible to bear the necessary pain for a continual growth in maturity and sanctity. One's ability to pray and love

God can ordinarily be measured by the willingness with which we renounce the pleasures of food and drink.

Lust

Closely akin to gluttony is lust. This is the exaggerated desire for the pleasures of sex. Only one who has solved the problem of sexuality is able to have a proper love for God and others. An excessive fear of sex is very nearly as bad as an exaggerated love of it. The intensity of the suffering frequently required to bring sexuality under control is most helpful in giving us a true picture of the extent of our egocentricity. During the struggle with sexual temptations we will be confronted with a thousand different aspects of our egotism. Much help from God and our fellow human beings is usually needed to help us fight our way through the intricacies of sensuality to the freedom of true love. In our efforts to control the instinctive desires of sex, we must be careful not to develop a false attitude. Sex is not something evil but a power for good, provided it is used in the proper way. Married people as well as single people need to practice constraint in this matter; otherwise, they will become enslaved to it. Everyone must learn how to unite the physical attraction to a truly spiritual and unselfish love for the other person. Sex is one of those vital energies that must never be merely repressed. Either we find a legitimate outlet for its energy by means of spiritual love or it will fill our whole life with obsessive drives, fears, anxieties, egotism and brutality. For the celibate person this outlet must be found in a life of all-out love and loving service for one's brothers and sisters.

Sloth

In the efforts necessary for a life of loving service for others, another hindrance will be found in the tendency to sloth. St. Thomas rather neatly defines sloth as the evil sadness that overtakes us at the prospect of the hard labor required to attain something good. Every one of us has experienced this spiritual laziness, probably more often than we care to admit. In this second aeon, no fault is overcome, no virtue acquired, without much effort. If we do not attain the maturity and sanctity that God has destined for us, it will be due, among other things, to our sloth. This distorted love of self is particularly harmful when it concerns our religious duties. Our prayer life becomes boring, tiresome and full of distractions. A state of lukewarmness renders our whole spiritual life barren. A host of other faults flow from sloth: cowardice in the face of duty; procrastination of everything that is difficult or requires effort; discouragement at the effort required for virtue; resentment for those who interfere with our self-centered life; bitterness towards God who asks so much of us; loss of enthusiasm for the higher values of life. A lifetime of strenuous effort is required to attain the love that is abused by sloth.

Envy

Another form of evil sadness is that which we feel toward the success of others. It is called envy. Having an exaggerated love of ourselves, we consider the good fortune of our rivals an affront to our own feelings of superiority. This resentment is especially strong if someone apparently less talented or less deserving than ourselves happens to be more successful than we have been. We experience deep pain whenever we hear others being praised and we do all in our power to depreciate that other person, both in our own judgment and in the opinion of others. If unchecked, envy turns into a hatred that may stop at nothing to destroy the reputation of the one who has outstripped us. Criticism, detraction, calumny, backbiting are some of the means used to tear down the good name of the other person. Sometimes the reason for envy is our own lack of security or refusal to put forth all the effort expected of us. None of us should be quick to deny the presence of envy in ourselves. It is very clever in concealing its presence from ourselves and finding some other reason to justify our opposition to the other person. Much criticism of others is motivated by this false love of self. With effort to cooperate with God's grace we can hope to transform our warped love of self into a sincere love of others.

Evil Anger

The last form of the abuse of love is that of anger, which is the desire to attack violently anyone who is a threat to us. There is a legitimate anger to be used against real evil. It becomes an evil when it is uncontrolled or when it is used for egotistical purposes. It is often an indication of our own lack of inner peace and security. We react violently to anyone who poses a threat to the high estimate we have of our own excellence or who threatens the precarious hold we have on our possessions. At other times, anger is an attempt to repair by revenge a loss of face suffered at the hands of another. If we are deeply insecure, we will be unable to tolerate any humiliation, defeat or sign of weakness. The more lacking in inner confidence, the more we will attack the one who threatens our freedom. If we are afraid to attack the actual one who is a threat to us, we will turn unreasonably to some other person nearby, usually a helpless inferior and vent our rage on that person. Often this rage will be for some really unimportant, nonsensical reason.

Any number of things can arouse evil anger in us, but in every case it is an indication of an abuse of love. Usually it is something within us that is disturbing us but we are afraid to face up to the real problem, so we project our wrath upon some likely victim who happens to cross our path. This often is someone who has a similar fault and the presence of this person is an unconscious reminder of our own failures. The first step in conquering anger is to take seriously the things that disturb us in others and try to see where we might be guilty of the same fault. The next step is to show the proper patience and love in transforming our fault into something good. With strenuous efforts on our part we will be able to turn the energy behind our anger into a powerful force of love. People with violent tempers are those who are capable of intense love, provided they will use God's grace in bringing about a metanoia in themselves.

The Ten Commandments

Each abuse of the Ten Commandments of Moses will always be motivated by one of the capital sins enumerated in this chapter. One reason so many people fail to reform their lives is because they keep hacking away at the external actions of sin as found in the ten Mosaic commandments, but fail to go to the root of the sin. This root will always be one or the other of the capital sins listed above. Unless the root is exposed, admitted and its energy transformed into love, we will never succeed in overcoming our faults. Therefore, when we go to confession in the Sacrament of Penance, we should not be content to list all the times we have broken one or other of the Ten Commandments. Rather, we should talk about root causes of our sins as found in the capital sins. Then we should discuss with the priest what we propose to do to change the direction of the energy that has been used for evil so that henceforth we will use this energy in pursuit of love of God and others.

REFLECTION AND DISCUSSION

1. How is my attachment to the things of the world holding me back from God?

2. In what areas am I trying to satisfy God by giving external actions rather than pursuing a loving relationship with Him?

CHAPTER 7

Obstacles to Grace and their Remedies

Traditionally the three great obstacles on our journey of faith have been called the world, the flesh, and the devil. I speak of them as the "three P's": possessions, pleasure, power. All three are creations of God and therefore are good if they are kept in their proper place. The problem is that they are so desirable and attractive that we have a tendency to idolize and worship them. Instead of seeing them as the limited, created goods that they are, we are tempted to make them into absolute goods and thus they replace God as the ultimate goal of our life. We make a god out of a limited good and become guilty of idolatry in our attitude toward it.

Possessions, pleasure, and power offer us a limited security in a very insecure world. Actually insecurity is an essential element of our creatureliness. However, it is not at all comfortable to be insecure. Therefore, we are constantly on the lookout for anything that can give us a feeling of security. Faith and trust in God are meant to be our ultimate security on earth. However, when we are lacking in trust in God, we have a tendency to look for anything that seems to offer a solution to our insecurity. For example, money or possessions offer a limited security to our earthly life. Therefore, they easily become the number one priority in our life. The more money and possessions we can call our own, the more secure we imagine we will be. Bodily pleasure is a second way of gaining a security upon earth. If our body is content with pleasure, we no longer feel insecure. Third, the possession of power over others, over nature, over ourselves, over the future, and over the world can easily become the idols which we worship. If we have power, we no longer feel weak and insecure. Another word for power is freedom, the freedom to do whatever we choose to do. Still another word for power is pride where we exalt our freedom above the freedom of God and make our will supreme rather than God's will. By means of one or more of these "three P's", we attempt to find a false, earthly security rather than find our security in God.

It is interesting to note that the "three P's" involve the three basic relationships around which our whole life on earth revolves. Pleasure has to do with ourselves, especially our bodies. Possessions have to do with our relationship with our neighbor. Power concerns our attitude toward God. When we worship power, we are attempting to steal from God the omnipotence S/He enjoys and make ourselves into an absolute power. When we worship pleasure and make it one of our supreme concerns in life, we have made a little god of our body. When we worship possessions and make the acquisition of money and earthly goods the supreme goal of life, we will usually fail in our duties of love and service to our neighbor.

The three temptations of Jesus during his sojourn in the desert may be seen as an attempt by Satan to get Jesus to make an absolute good out of pleasure, possessions, and power. Actually these God-given powers were to be used only to help others and carry out his ministry as the Messiah. The first temptation to turn the stones into bread was a subtle way of tempting Jesus to use the miraculous powers he possessed to satisfy his own bodily pleasure. The second temptation, according to the Gospel of Luke, was Satan's offer to give Jesus possession of all the earth in exchange for Jesus' worship of Satan. The worship of Satan seems to be the price we must pay when we make acquisition of money and earthly possessions the supreme goal of our life. The third temptation was a subtle appeal to the power over nature that Jesus enjoyed. It was to be manifested by floating down into the Temple Square from the highest pinnacle of the temple. Showing off his superhuman powers would have been a wrong use of power and an act of pride on Jesus' part. Therefore Jesus rejected this as well as the other suggestions from Satan. No matter how much power we may have, this power is never to be used selfishly but only in accord with the will of God. The same is true of pleasure and possessions.

Because they are so attractive to us, they easily become our masters. We begin to serve them as our gods instead of the true God. There is such a distortion of truth that when we make any one of the "three P's" into absolute goals in our life, they cease to be good and become evil.

Because there is so much energy behind each of these three values when they become ultimate goals they take on the personality of evil spirits. These evil forces pose a threat to our earthly welfare as well as to our eternal salvation. When we absolutize any one of these three limited values we become possessed by their evil energy. A popular term for such evil possession is addiction. We become addicted to power, pleasure, or possessions. Every sin and evil in the world can be traced to addiction to one or the other of these "three

P's". Only God and God's will are to be loved absolutely. We must never love any created good or any creature in an absolute, unlimited way.

Capital sins are simply different ways of exaggerating the place of power, pleasure, and possessions in our life. Pride and anger are concerned with power. Sinful anger is present whenever we desire to do violence to anyone who poses a threat to our freedom and power. Gluttony, lust, and sloth are different ways our pursuit of pleasure goes astray. Gluttony exaggerates the value of food and drink; lust does the same for sexual pleasure; and sloth carries to extreme the desire for ease and comfort. Greed and envy involve our attitude toward earthly possessions. We are greedy when we exaggerate the value of earthly goods. We are envious when we begrudge others having more of this world's goods than we possess.

Forewarned is forearmed. Satan is very clever in the many subtle ways we are tempted to exaggerate the importance of pleasure, possessions, and power to our life. Since each of these "three P's" is actually something good and created by God for our benefit and use, it is easy to be deceived in our perception of how worthwhile and necessary is a too-dedicated pursuit of these goals. We are often tempted to make them into absolute goals around which our life revolves. We may put one or more of them ahead of God and thus we become guilty of idolatry or worship of false gods.

The Three Remedies

In the Gospel, Jesus told his apostles that there are certain evil spirits which can be cast out only by prayer and fasting (Matt 17:21). We need to add almsgiving to prayer and fasting and say that the only way to be delivered from a slavery or addiction to power, pleasure, or possessions is by the practice of the three remedies of prayer, fasting, and almsgiving. Through *prayer* we acknowledge our dependence upon God's power rather than our own power. Through *fasting* we bring under control our attraction to sensual pleasure. Through *almsgiving* we become detached from an excessive love of money and possessions. Our Christian tradition has constantly urged us to practice prayer, fasting, and almsgiving. Jesus speaks of all three of these remedies in the sixth chapter of St. Matthew's Gospel. Traditionally these have been the three practices which every Christian is urged to carry out each day of Lent. Actually, these three practices should be a daily touchstone or a simple test of conscience for anyone aspiring to a richer and fuller spirituality. Like the "three P's", these three remedies involve the three relationships of love around which our whole life should revolve. Prayer deals with having a good loving relationship with God. Fasting is directed toward a proper, balanced love of self. Almsgiving as a general term refers to all our duties of love of neighbor.

Prayer

Prayer enables us to keep the temptation to power under control. When we pray, we recognize God as the only one with absolute power and we submit our will and freedom to God's will. We might define prayer as anything that helps our relationship of love with God. As such it does not require words or any special form or method. The goal of our prayer-life is to have the thought and desire of God always before us every waking moment of our life. Brother Lawrence's book, *The Practice of the Presence of God*, is a good example of our life's goal for prayer.

The accomplishment of a total union with God is the work of our whole lifetime. It is a task to which we need to address our attention every single day. We will never be able to carry out our duties of love of neighbor and a proper love of self unless we have the necessary help from God that comes through prayer. The psychiatrist Gerald May has written an excellent book, *Addiction and Grace,* in which he shows that it is impossible to overcome our addictions without the grace and help of God. He believes that many of us are unaware of the multiple addictions we have developed, and how these sap energy from our growth in wholeness.

The most significant result of each experience of prayer is an increase in the virtue of humility. By humility we mean a constant, conscious recognition of our total dependence on God and our total helplessness as a creature apart from God. Humility is synonymous with authenticity and truth and it is the basic foundation upon which all the other virtues depend. It addresses the problem of power and personal freedom and is the direct opposite of pride and the exaggerated love of one's own power. Humility is being not proud or haughty, not arrogant or over-assertive; it expresses a spirit of deference or submission. Humility and prayer are so closely connected that it is impossible to pray well without humility and it is impossible to have humility without prayer. Prayer is the only antidote which will counteract the poison in our system which results from an excessive concern with power, pleasure, or possessions. A direct result of prayer is an increase of trust in God. Such trust in God is the only real, lasting security possible here on earth. In prayer we freely choose to trust God's power. When we neglect to pray, we choose to trust our own power to decide and to act. God indeed has shared with us some of His power and freedom. But, these are limited gifts and we are guilty of pride when we choose to act as though our human freedom was an absolute power. Therefore, pride is a form of idolatry. We make a god out of our power to choose and our freedom to act. We put more trust in ourself than we do in God. Whereas, by prayer we choose to center our life in God.

Prayer had a very important place in the life of Jesus upon earth. He spent whole nights in prayer. His whole life was centered in God, his Heavenly Father. He trusted in the power of God rather than in his own human powers. He insisted that his disciples have a similar trust in God and Jesus taught them how to express this trust in God through prayer. The Lord's Prayer is an example of such trust in God.

Jesus' temptation to cast himself down from the pinnacle of the temple was a temptation to trust his own human power as an absolute power instead of recognizing its limitations. Jesus' reply to this temptation was, "You shall not put the Lord your God to the test." Each day we fail to pray, each time we give into the temptation of pride, each time we trust in our own freedom and power rather than in God, we put God to the test. In other words, we tempt the Lord our God.

Almsgiving

As a generic term, almsgiving is synonymous with love of neighbor. It is much broader than merely giving money or possessions to the poor. We need to deepen our understanding of our possessions to include, all the gifts and blessings of our life: our time, our talents, our energies, our intelligence, our experiences, as well as our material possessions. Almsgiving is concerned with all our relationships with others, and if it is practiced properly, it will prevent us from making a god out of any of our possessions and blessings. By almsgiving we willingly share our gifts with others. We recognize that we are merely stewards of the possessions that happen to be listed in our name. One day we will have to render an account to God as to whether we have used all of these gifts to do the greatest possible good to everyone. We have an obligation to take care of our personal needs as well as those of our family and dependents. But, it is against justice for us to have luxuries and an over-abundance of the goods of this world while others starve and are deprived of even the barest necessities. By almsgiving we try to bring about a balance between the "haves" and the "have nots" of the world. If it is practiced generously, we will never make a god out of money or any of the things of this world.

We should see our relationship of love with others as our ministry of loving service to them. Jesus says that our charity toward our neighbor will be the telltale sign by which we will be known as his disciples (Jn 13:35).

The goal of almsgiving is to fulfill as perfectly as possible the new commandment of love of neighbor which Jesus gave to his disciples at the Last Supper. "A new commandment I give you that you should love one another as I have loved you" (John 13:34). Webster's dictionary defines alms as "something given freely to relieve the poor." If we think of every human being as being poor and needy, then almsgiving is a good word to describe all that is involved in loving others as Jesus loved his disciples.

The purpose of almsgiving is to bring under control the very legitimate desire for possessions which God has implanted in our nature for the sake of self-survival. However, like the other two desires, power and pleasure, the desire for possessions has a tendency to become an absolute value instead of a limited good. When we give into this temptation we make an idol out of our earthly possessions. According to Luke's Gospel, the price to pay for making possessions the supreme goal of life is the worship of Satan (Luke 4:6- 7). Our American culture seems to have made money and earthly possessions the supreme goal of life. The love of money and the things that money can buy is at the root of much of the evil and violence in the world today. In fact, we are willing to go to war in order to protect our American way of life. Living in such a culture, each of us is bound to be somewhat contaminated by this excessive regard for money and the things money can buy.

Fasting

Fasting is the general term for all those acts of self-discipline by which we bring our desires for sensual pleasure under reasonable control. When used specifically, fasting refers to moderation in the use of food and drink. In the Gospel Jesus puts fasting on a par with prayer as a means to rid ourselves of evil. For instance, when the apostles asked Jesus why they were unable to cast out an evil spirit, Jesus replied that there were certain evil spirits that could be cast out only by prayer and fasting (Matthew 17: 21). A more modern word for fasting would be self-discipline, which advocates keeping the proper balance in all of our desires and appetites. It does not mean that we should torture ourselves or that God enjoys seeing us suffer or being miserable and unhappy. God wants us to enjoy life on earth but for this to happen, everything must be done in moderation. Pleasure is one of God's creations for our benefit. However, like possessions and power, the pursuit of earthly pleasure is meant to be a limited good. When we make pleasure an absolute good, we make a god out of it. St. Paul says that such persons make their belly their god (Phil 3:19).

The very first temptation Jesus had during his sojourn in the desert was to gratify his hunger by turning stones into bread. Jesus' response to Satan was, "Not by bread alone does a person live." Jesus is not condemning the pleasures of food. Jesus enjoyed eating and drinking to the extent that his enemies accused him of being a glutton and an indulger in wine. Rather Jesus is reminding us that bodily pleasure is a limited good and not an absolute one. Because the attraction toward sensual pleasure is so powerful, we need to place a restraint upon its enjoyment. The goal of fasting and self-discipline is to establish a proper attitude of love toward ourselves and our own needs. To discern God's will for us we can study the example of Jesus and other good and holy persons and then by prayer and experience decide what is best and proper for our present situation.

The successful accomplishment of the three tasks of prayer, fasting, and almsgiving will result in decentering from excessive concern for oneself and a recentering of our whole life in God, God's will, God's plan and destiny for us and for the whole world. It will also result in at least an equal concern for the welfare and needs of our neighbor. If we wish to become totally Christ-like, then a Christ-like practice of the above three activities will result in an even greater concern for the wellbeing of others than for our own well-being. This willingness to sacrifice our welfare for the benefit of others is what Jesus means when he uses the symbolism of the cross. "Whoever wishes to be my disciple must deny his very self, take up his cross each day, and follow in my steps" (Luke 9:23).

Obstacles to Grace and Their Remedies

	DEMONS	ANTIDOTES
THREE DESERT DEMONS	Pleasure Possessions Power	Fasting Almsgiving Prayer
SEVEN TRADITIONAL DEMONS	Pride Greed Envy Sloth Lust Gluttony Anger	Humility Detachment Love Sacrifice Charity, Purity Self-Discipline Self-Discipline, Meekness
FIFTEEN MODERN DEMONS	Negativity Fear Ignorance Confusion Insecurity Mediocrity Deceit Procrastination Selfishness Qualified Love Excess Violence Cowardice Injustice Credit Cards	Positive Attitude Trust Education Simplicity Faith Generosity Authenticity Sacrament of Present Moment Unselfishness Unconditional Love Balance, Moderation Non-Violent Love Confrontation Justice Payment in Full Monthly

REFLECTION AND DISCUSSION

1. Take a moment and consider how you spend your time, your energy, your money, and your worry. Refer to the list at the end of this chapter and select one or two of your most tenacious demons, either traditional or modern. Write a personal plan for bringing your excessive affection for one of God's good gifts into greater balance in your life. Include measurable objectives, and share your plan with a trusted friend or spiritual director.

In reviewing your progress over time, remember to celebrate your growth and to incorporate new insights into a revised growth plan on a regular basis.

CHAPTER 8

Conversion of Evil into Good

We often try to repress an evil tendency which we find in ourselves but this is not always good. If it is repressed out of sight of our consciousness, this fault regresses into the unconscious where we no longer have any control over it. There it festers and corrupts our inner being, filling us with unhealthy fears and anxieties. The proper, but more difficult, procedure is to enter into combat with each of our faults until we have succeeded in transforming them into true virtues. This is primarily a task of learning how to direct the energy behind the fault into the proper channel of love. Paradoxically, the more powerful the undesirable tendency, the stronger are the possibilities of great love within us. A strong personality is capable of immense good as well as immense evil, and it is to be preferred to a weak mind and heart that is less capable of producing any results either good or evil. Instead of being disturbed by some grievous temptation, we should rejoice that the Lord has given us a strong character.

There are many examples of how we can redirect the energy of evil into a new channel of goodness. By refusing to pass judgment upon someone who has done evil, we are able to change the direction of our energy from anger to mercy and forgiveness. By refusing to seek revenge against someone who has harmed us, we can redirect the energy of anger into mercy and love. The energy that is used to hate and work violence upon others is the exact same energy that may be used to show love and forgiveness to those persons. It is a matter of using our freedom and the power of our will to choose to show love rather than hate.

Each of us receives all the help we need to incarnate our nature into the life of grace. We must cooperate with God's grace. There is need of a great deal of patience with our faults; but if we persevere to the end, we shall be saved. It is to be expected that we will fall many times as we climb the mountain of perfection. After each fall we resume the climb, never allowing discouragement to overwhelm us. Our heavenly Father/Mother is quick to forgive, provided we are willing to rise and keep climbing. Regardless of the past, God will give us the grace here and now to make a new start. Our best assurance for the future is to be generous with the Lord today.

The conversion of evil into good is not an easy task and the greater one's potential for sanctity, the more difficult this work will be. It is a job that is never finished this side of the grave. For most of us, it continues beyond this life into purgatory. However, there is no reason why we should wait until after death to complete the work of our sanctity. God desires that we should attain sanctity here upon earth before we die.

The conversion of faults into virtues is called "metanoia" or penance. We are called to reform, to change, and repent. The Good News of salvation can be accepted only by those who are willing to undergo a real conversion of their hearts toward good. This was the message of Isaiah to the chosen people of the Old Testament and is also the message of Jesus to the community of God's people under the new covenant of love. This spirit of penance or metanoia has been the constant theme of Christian preachers throughout the centuries.

Metanoia implies two things: a turning away from the evil toward which one's energies have been directed and a positive redirecting of all our powers toward some good. The legitimate recipients of our love may be God, our neighbor, ourselves, and the world. But all these loves must be according to the proper order and balance that God wills for us. God's will must be the center of our life and efforts; everything else must be oriented around this. It is not easy to attain this balance, but the struggle will be the cross that brings salvation to us.

The first of the powers that needs to be converted is what St. Paul calls the "flesh." "The flesh lusts against the Spirit and the Spirit against the flesh" (Gal 5:17). In the original Greek, the word used by St. Paul for this evil tendency is "sarx." In the Gospels, a further distinction is made between the flesh (sarx) and the spirit (pneuma): "the spirit (pneuma) indeed is willing, but the flesh (sarx) is weak" (Mt 26:41). We might define sarx as anything in our nature that is hostile to God and the indwelling of the Holy Spirit. It is misleading when we translate sarx as flesh, since this implies that our body is evil. More clearly stated, sarx is the propensity toward sin as a result of our fallen human nature as opposed to our spiritual nature which yearns for the things of God. The hostile powers of the sarx are part of our human nature with its limitations and lusts for power, pleasure, and possessions.

Like the Hebrews in Egypt, all of us have been born into a condition of slavery to the sarx of our human nature. We come into the world wearing the chain of slavery because the sins of our ancestors have implanted within us a hostility to God and God's will. Baptism does not completely free us from this condition but gives us a pledge of the Holy Spirit to convert the energy of the sarx into authentic love. By cooperating with the graces of the sacraments, we can gradually transform these inclinations of the will toward evil into the energies of love. If we are conquered by the sarx, it will not be because God has failed to do His part; it will be because we have failed to cooperate with God's graces.

The aversion to acquiescence to God that dwells in each of us is encouraged by the hostile powers present in others. The more the other person has consented to corruption, the more contagious his/her attitude will be and the sooner we will be influenced by it. When we are struggling with the inclinations of our own sarx, it is no help to come into the presence of someone who has long since made a decision against God and God's will. If we are on the fence and unwilling to make a commitment of love, a meeting with an enemy of God can easily cause us to reject God. On the other hand, if we have already thrown our energies into doing the will of God, we can expect an open conflict with any enemies of God that we may encounter. There are real spiritual enemies who try to lead us astray, but we remain masters of our destiny and can decide what we wish to do with our life.

Jesus tells us that all hostility to God is centered in a definite reality whom he calls "the prince of this world" (Jn 14:30). This enemy of God is also called Satan who along with the other evil forces are the "world rulers of darkness" (Eph 6:12). According to St. Paul, at Baptism, God "rescued us from the power of darkness and brought us into the Kingdom of his beloved son" (Col 1:13). The power of Satan, however, is still present on earth and will only be destroyed when Christ comes the final time to complete the Kingdom of God in the third aeon. During this present "between time", our adversary, the devil, "as a roaring lion, goes about seeking someone to devour" (I Pt 5:8). "Woe to the earth and the sea, because the devil has gone down in great wrath, knowing that he has but a short time" (Rev 12:12).

Satan looks for allies among those worldly people who have given vent to the energies of their sarx. Through them God's adversary seeks to lead us away from the path of love. If we can imagine the combined hostility to God that dwells in the hearts of people living in the world, we will understand what Jesus meant when he calls the world the enemy of those who have allowed their spiritual nature to develop and grow. "The world has hated them, because they are not of the world even as I am not of the world" (Jn 17:14).

Just as we must make a distinction between our own "flesh" and our "sarx", so we must distinguish the "world" created by God which is good from the combined animosity (sarx) of the people of the world. It is this latter "world" which is our enemy. Just as we have the task of converting our own aversions into love, so we must help others convert their evil tendencies into good. The best method is to struggle with our own inclinations (or addictions) and to transform this energy into authentic love. Even if we do not succeed with others, the effort expended will protect us from being led astray and will help us complete the work of sanctification within us.

Our hearts must go out in love to those who carry a hostility to God. Even if they cause us much suffering, we must continue to love them, pray for them, and seek to help them transform their energies of hate into love. From the example of Christ in his passion, we see how the power of love can turn the hatred of the world into an instrument of salvation. Through the love of Jesus, the greatest crime in history, the murder of the God-Man, became the very act that saved us. If we follow the example of Jesus, we can transform the hatred of our persecutors into a power for salvation, both for our enemies and many others, as well as for ourselves.

The more we have succeeded in sublimating our own lower nature into love, the better able we will be to help our brothers and sisters. If we are willing to take up our cross each day and follow Christ to Calvary, we will have made a substantial contribution to the salvation and resurrection of the world.

We have God's repeated promises in the Sacred Scriptures that good, not evil, will triumph in the end. Final victory is assured; it awaits only the loving cooperation of many persons of good will. Ten good people would have been sufficient to save the cities of Sodom and Gomorrah (Gn 18:32).

REFLECTION AND DISCUSSION

1. How do you typically react when those around are united in their judgment of another person, known or unknown to you? How do you express your divergent

view? How do you engage them in considering alternative positive responses which lead to life?

2. What evil tendency plagues you and how can you work to transform it by God's grace into good?

CHAPTER 9

Progress in the Natural Virtues

Throughout life, during our journey of faith, it is important that we emphasize the positive rather than the negative. Both growth in virtue and the conquering of faults are necessary, but the greater effort should be given to the virtues. Since every fault is a misdirected virtue, any progress in the virtues will result in a corresponding weakening of our faults. We will need to understand, develop, and practice the natural and supernatural virtues. The supernatural virtues are faith, hope, and charity. For these we are dependent upon the grace of God along with our cooperation. The natural virtues to be covered in this chapter are humility, justice, courage, prudence, temperance, and art. We also need God's help to practice these virtues, but we want to emphasize here the necessity of our own effort.

Since nature and grace normally should be balanced within us, we should aim at attaining a perfection of all the virtues needed for maturity and sanctity. None of the virtues can be separated from the others; any progress in one will make easier the practice of the others. Our goal in life is the incarnation of our whole nature into Christ. A constant stream of grace is needed to accomplish this transformation and this will come to us through the sacraments and prayer, our own prayers and the prayers of our friends. Without God and our sisters and brothers, it would be a hopeless task to attempt to reach wholeness.

It is only by the cooperation of God, the community, and ourselves, that the goal of the Kingdom of God is attained.

Virtue of Humility

Among the natural virtues, the first and most important is humility. It is the footing or foundation upon which all the other virtues, both natural and supernatural, will be built. Humility means the willingness to face the full truth about ourselves, to see ourselves as God sees us. A synonym for humility is honesty or authenticity. If one is leading a life of deception, this absence of honesty in one's personality will be the cause of physical, mental, emotional, and spiritual troubles. In this sense, humility or honesty is more essential and important than goodness. God loves the honest sinner much more than the dishonest, self-righteous "saint." Jesus severely condemned the absence of this virtue of humility in the Pharisees.

Having humility means acceptance of both our virtues and our vices, our fears and weaknesses, our limitations and our failures. Not only are we willing to admit these things to ourselves, we are willing that others recognize them, and we will openly reveal them whenever the occasion demands. On the other hand, we will also admit to the blessings, graces and everything else that is good in our life. We will always be aware that this goodness is due to God's mercy and we will thank God accordingly.

We are usually less good than we imagine ourselves to be. Great pain is felt as we face up to the unpleasant facts about our character which are seen by others but not by ourselves. It would be harmful to our growth in sanctity to be given a total revelation of our faults at one sitting. The first step is to face up to the probability that there indeed are evil tendencies in our inner being of which we are presently unaware. There is a need to bring them gradually to the surface of consciousness, decontaminate them, and then transform them into virtues. If we are humble, we will face the fact that we are capable of committing every sin or crime that we have ever heard of. When we acknowledge the truth about our own evil tendencies, we will never despise others, no matter how terrible they are. Remembering our own sins of the past and the pride present in our heart, we will go out in love to every sinner, even the worst.

In the process of attaining humility and honesty, we will endure many crises. In the tension that results from the confrontation of our pride and dishonesty, there is danger of a breakdown of our will to live and grow in maturity. It is often impossible to face the full truth about our sinfulness. We need the encouragement of a friend who admits the truth about us, yet still loves us, believes in us, and is willing to help us transform our sarx into virtue. Without this encouragement, there is danger of our falling victim to despair. This friend, who is perhaps a spiritual director or a spiritual friend or prayer partner, accepts the full truth about us and yet will have high hopes for our ultimate victory over evil and the attainment of sanctity. This friend can help us to the realization that God loves us even as we are and that with divine help it is not too late to achieve maturity and sanctity. Without such a friend, few are able to face the truth about themselves and survive. The confidence that is needed to keep us progressing towards sanctity comes indeed from God but nearly always through the love of a human friend.

Virtue of Justice

Justice is giving to everyone what is due to them. St. Thomas Aquinas puts all of our religious duties to God under the virtue of justice as in the norm of right order. They comprise the service which is due to God by the very nature of our creatureliness. Justice toward God means to show reverence, awe, respect, obedience, love, service, and cooperation with God's will.

Justice toward our fellow human beings means to do all in our power to see that they have all that is due to them as human beings. This would include the opportunity to work and earn a livelihood, health care, education in addition to the necessities of life such as food, clothing, and shelter. Justice to others also includes recognition of their freedom as persons, their need for love, security, peace, absence of violence, etc.

There is also a justice which we owe to ourselves. We have a duty to take proper care of our physical, psychological, and spiritual health. We owe it to ourselves to develop our potential for good as highly as possible.

When the Gospel calls Joseph a just man, it is the same as saying Joseph was a holy man. In the New Testament, justice, righteousness, and holiness are synonyms meaning the same thing.

Our Lord tells us in the Beatitudes that every Christian should have an incessant hunger and thirst for justice. Those persons who are not vitally interested in bringing justice into all the areas of life cannot be considered true Christians. The Church asks us to work to bring justice into international relations, undeveloped nations, to the poor, to the downtrodden and persecuted people all over the world. We are urged to help eradicate racism, ethnic prejudices, and the other evils which separate and divide the human family.

Virtue of Courage

Aquinas defines courage as the virtue which strengthens us to do what reason dictates as right and to overcome the fear of danger and toil. Courage is not the absence of fear; it is acting in spite of fear. Without courage we could never face the truth about ourselves and tackle the many difficult tasks needed to reach wholeness. Both maturity and sanctity are fundamentally the proper exercise of love, and the greatest enemy of love is not malice but fear. As long as our hearts are filled with fear, there will be no real progress in loving. Courage is the virtue that conquers fear. It is essential to any growth in wholeness.

With courage we are willing to try new things and take the chances needed to go forward into the unknown future. Each of us must cut a new path through the jungle of worldly life to the mountain of holiness. The life of each of us is a new day holding out the exciting promise of things that have never been accomplished in the history of the world. Every person is meant to be a pioneer, boldly taking control of one's destiny and venturing into new areas. There is today a special need of this pioneering spirit among all Christians as we seek to discover God's plans for the world, the church, and ourselves.

Where do we find the heroic courage needed to be a saint and pioneer? Courage will come first from God through the virtue of hope, which is the supernatural incarnation of natural courage. Second, it will come from the courage and inspiration of friends, either living or dead. Reading the lives of the saints and meditating on the tremendous courage they showed in trying new things, in overcoming fear and in enduring suffering can be a great help. We can learn from the experiences of others but there must never be any slavish imitation. Each of us is a unique creation of God.

It is also possible to gain courage from the realization that the driving force behind our fears and cowardice is the misdirected energy of love. We fear being rebuffed. We can overcome our fear of disapproval, failure, and loneliness if we intensify our charity toward others. With the help of God's grace, the help of our friends, and our common sense, we will find the wisdom needed for a courage that is daring but not foolhardy.

Virtue of Prudence

Prudence may be defined as the common sense that enables us to make the right decisions about what to do or say. God has given each of us the freedom to assume responsibility for our life and actions. God will also give us the grace to develop the prudence needed for our vocation in life, but this grace does not work without our cooperation. Through study, experience, and hard work we should develop the common sense needed to make the right and best decisions regarding the conduct of our life.

It is possible to go to extremes on both sides of prudence. We may be either lacking in common sense or perhaps too cautious, using this circumspection as an excuse for inactivity and cowardice. It is also wrong to throw all caution to the wind and become reckless in our decisions. Through the Gift of Counsel, the Holy Spirit will give us the grace to perfect the virtue of prudence and the wisdom of good judgment.

Virtue of Temperance

Every virtue is a balance between two extremes. Temperance is the virtue that curbs these extremes without destroying their power for good. It is like the harness and the bridle which make it possible for us to use the energies of a high-spirited horse without breaking its spirit. Through self-control and self-denial one can harness one's passions and powers to do good and to harm no one. All of our faculties, both spiritual and physical, are gifts of God to be used in the service of our neighbor and ourselves. Because of sin, these powers have a tendency to usurp their proper position as servants of our will and thus become independent of all control. The hard work of discipline is needed to achieve moderation and balance among these warring factions within our nature.

In the first twenty-five years of one's life particularly, self-discipline is to be learned, practiced, perfected. Care must be taken not to kill our creative energies but rather to develop and control them. To weak and cowardly souls it often seems safer to repress them, especially if they continue to give one trouble. Nevertheless, it is in the very struggle to live under tension that we will find the strength to progress into the wholeness of maturity and sanctity. By the second half of life, there should be enough good habits of self-discipline established so that we no longer need be afraid of our passions of anger, hate, and our desire for power and control but can give our attention to the higher virtues, especially that of charity.

Virtue of Art

St. Thomas Aquinas says in his work *Man and the Conduct of Life*, that art is the virtue that gives us the right judgment of the things to be made. All of us need to develop our talents of creativity, since every human being has the vocation of an artist. We all are called to be co-creators with God in refashioning the things of earth until we have formed the New Creation of the Kingdom of God. The world, as we have it today, is the raw material out of which the reign of God is to be accomplished. The Divine Creator depends upon us to cooperate with Him in creating the new heaven and new earth. Each of us has been given specific talents of creativity, and it is our task to develop these talents to their full capacity. In addition to receiving God's helping grace, we must cooperate by studying under good artists who have developed their facility of making things good and beautiful to express the transcendental beauty of God.

The greatest of all arts is the direction of human beings toward maturity and sanctity. The raw material in this instance is the most precious of all God's creations—the human person with a spiritual soul and a physical body. All of us have the responsibility to be our brother's and sister's keeper. Therefore, we are called in one way or another to work with people and to help them reach the wholeness for which they are destined.

Like all artists, spiritual directors must have great respect and reverence for the material with which they work. We must not try to force others to do things which may not be part of their destiny. We will show consideration for their freedom and avoid dishonesty and artificiality with them. We will be patient and willing to work long hours in helping them without expecting recompense. By studying the behavior of a really first-class artist, and the Greatest Artist of all, Our Lord Jesus Christ, we can learn much of how we should act toward others to help them fulfill and actualize their creative potential for beauty and for love.

REFLECTION AND DISCUSSION

1. The natural virtues are enumerated as humility, justice, courage, prudence, temperance, and art. Of these, select one for focus. With regard to achieving balance in your life, where do you stand in relationship to the virtue? Where have you made progress and what work can you do to continue? What role are you willing to have someone else play in helping you achieve progress?

2. Within our culture, what does the virtue of justice mean? How does this definition parallel or differ from the virtue of justice as defined by Christ?

CHAPTER 10

Growth in Wholeness and Maturity

The rhythm of life is a cycle of birth, growth, death, and rebirth. For us to reach wholeness, it is necessary that we die again and again to the things of the past and the present so that we can be born again on a higher level of life. Each of these deaths is a fork in the road at which we are given the freedom to choose a higher and seemingly more difficult way of life or to regress to a lower, less demanding way of existence. The decisions we make during these crises will determine both the physical and spiritual course of our life. At these critical junctures we are masters of our own destiny, capable of deciding the direction of our life. Each time we sacrifice something that is near and dear to us, and choose a better way of life, we are paying the necessary price for growth in wholeness.

Sacred Scripture gives a name to this death of the old life and resurrection to a new life. In the original Greek this is called "metanoia," which may be translated as conversion, change of direction, penance, or renewal. The verb form means "to repent," "to do penance," "to be converted," "to be renewed." In the Gospels, our Lord and St. John the Baptist urgently recommend metanoia as the way to enter the Kingdom of God.

In the Acts of the Apostles, St. Peter, St. Paul, and the other apostles speak of faith and metanoia as two dispositions necessary for baptism and the life of grace. Faith is the positive side of conversion. Having turned away from evil or the lesser good, we must make a commitment to something better. St. Paul describes the process as the death of the "old man" of sin and the resurrection of the "new man" of grace. However, to experience this death and resurrection at baptism is not enough. Only by experiencing many deaths and enjoying many resurrections are maturity and sanctity reached. Ideally, growth in wholeness of nature and growth in grace should progress side by side. In practice, they are seldom together. However, one's continued progress toward natural maturity and wholeness makes it easier to endure the needed metanoia for growth in supernatural sanctity.

It is impossible to bring our psychological or spiritual life to a dead stop, without any movement forward or backward. Whenever we stop growing toward a greater maturity, we start to regress deep in our being. In a natural way, these regressions show themselves in psychosomatic illnesses, disturbing dreams, a general lack of peace and confidence in ourselves, anxieties and neurotic fears. Our hearts dry up, become cold and hard; we are unable to go out to others in genuine love. Our prayers become full of distractions, and our relationship with God lacks enthusiasm and joy. We become pessimistic about the future, the world, the Church, even the providence of God. Our efforts to do good seem useless and a sour, bitter, negative attitude begins to infiltrate our whole life.

On the other hand, if we are willing to suffer through each crisis and keep going toward something higher, a new and glorious resurrection will occur. At the point of greatest suffering, all may seem to be lost. We will be called upon to give up certain things and to go forward to something new. At each critical point it is to be expected that sometimes we will take the wrong road, make a faulty decision, even after weighing both sides carefully. If a wrong choice is made, we must humbly admit our mistake, withdraw gracefully, and then look again for the right road. Never should our past mistakes cause us to retreat into a shell or make us unwilling to take new chances when another decision has to be made. In the pattern of growth toward wholeness there will be many trials and failures. The important thing is that we keep trying to go higher and higher, progressing toward wholeness and holiness.

In order to attain our goal of sanctity and maturity, it is necessary that we be able to control *four fears: fear of God, fear of the world, fear of others, fear of ourselves.* These fears must be replaced by a well-ordered and balanced love, which will give us the confidence to deal properly with them. "God is love and he who abides in love abides in God and God in him. Our love is brought to perfection in this that we should have confidence on the day of judgment ... Love has no room for fear; perfect love casts out all fear and since fear has to do with punishment, love is imperfect in one who fears" (I Jn 4:16-18).

Yet, Sacred Scripture also says *"The Fear of the Lord* is the beginning of wisdom" (Ps 111:10). As in everything else, there is need of a balance between a healthy respect for God and love for God. God is both awesome and attractive and we always need to keep in mind these two sides of divine nature. When thinking of God's justice and holiness, we must also remember His divine goodness and love. An exaggerated fear of God may be due to faulty education or may indicate a weak and co-wardly personality. Regardless of the cause, extreme fear of committing sin and losing God results in a loss of freedom and a powerlessness to make decisions. We become prisoners of our fears, lacking the courage to launch out into the unknown future. Our growth is then curtailed and regression to a lower level of life begins.

An exaggerated *fear of the world* also prevents our progress towards sanctity and wholeness. There are those who mistake Christ's warnings concerning the world. It is true that there are powers at work in the world which are hostile to God and to our own best interests. However this does not mean that the world as such is evil. Anything that God creates is good and it is our task to discover this good and help to develop it into the fullness of its perfection. We should be fascinated with the wonderful things of God's creation but without becoming a slave to them. God created us to be lord of the universe and intends that all the creatures of nature be our servants. We are to respect and love these servants and use them according to the purposes for which God intended them, but never should we allow the world to control us through a slavish fear of it.

A third fear that hinders our making the right decisions for growth is *fear of our fellow human beings*. Instead of feeling inferior before others, we need to become conscious of our unity with all the members of the human family. We are children of the same heavenly parent and we all are struggling together toward the goal of wholeness. We need each other in our efforts to reach maturity and sanctity.

We should be humble and loving enough to ask for help without feeling that we have lost any of our human dignity. At the same time we should be ready to help others in their needs. Through situations of need and help we realize our creatureliness and our real solidarity with one another. We must strive to strike a balance between an exaggerated dependence on others and a proud independence of them. When something goes wrong, the primary concern should not be an effort to place the blame on someone, but rather for all of us to work together to remedy the situation. At one time or another we all have been guilty of wrongdoing; therefore, all of us are partly responsible for the troubles of the world.

A fourth fear to be overcome is an *egocentric fear of ourselves and of our ability to succeed.* We must have enough self-knowledge and enough confidence in our own worth to believe that with God's help we can reach the goal for which we were destined. Trusting ourselves to God and to the powers and talents of our inner self, we must allow God's providence to mold us according to God's own pattern. It may be quite different from what we, or others, have superficially judged to be best for us; yet we must courageously go forward toward an ever-higher goal.

To keep progressing toward the wholeness of nature and grace, it will be necessary for us to overcome many fears in regard to ourselves. Often the fear most difficult to conquer is the fear of our sexuality. It is often possible to judge one's growth in maturity by the facility with which one handles the precious gift of love according to the particular state of life in which one finds oneself. Both married and single people must learn the art of sublimating sexual attraction so that its power can be siphoned off into higher forms of love and service towards others. For those who lead a celibate life, physical attraction must be incarnated into spiritual love. When we have attained this ability, we usually lose that exaggerated fear of self which prevents growth in maturity.

In order to overcome these four fears, it is necessary to endure much struggle. Instead of running away from the difficulties of life, we should be grateful for them. Without problems and crises to be conquered, few of us would have the courage to attain the high goals God has destined for us. Our greatest and most constant struggle in life will always be to overcome fear and replace it with love: love of God, love of our neighbor, and a balanced love of ourselves and the world. We have been endowed by our Creator with an unlimited power to love. With the help of God and with constant effort on our part, it is possible to control this power and direct it toward its proper goals.

The Four Steps of Individuation

The resolution of our present worldwide crisis must first occur in the lives of individuals, one by one. As each of us finds the proper balance for the various relationships around which our life revolves, we move to a fuller maturity and understanding of the necessity of love toward all and among all.

There are four basic relationships that we need to bring to maturity and establish a proper balance between them. They are: our relationship with the various aspects of our own personality; our relationship with God; our relationship with other individual human beings; our relationship with the various groups, institutions, organizations to which we belong. Carl Jung, in his work *Memory, Dreams, and Reflections*, has suggested appropriate names for the maturity of each of these four relationships: authenticity, significance, transparency, and solidarity. Jung also maintains that the maturity for each one of us is unique and different from every other human being. He, therefore, called the whole process of maturation "individuation".

Authenticity

Our first task is to become authentic and honest with ourselves. Jesus says, "You shall know the truth and the truth will set you free" (Jn 8:32). Shakespeare in Hamlet urges: "to thine own self be true." Authenticity is a synonym for humility. It begins with self-knowledge but goes beyond knowledge to the establishment of a proper balance between all the conscious and unconscious faculties of our being.

Our first task is to accomplish the proper development of our ego. The ego includes all of our conscious faculties but is centered especially in the conscious human will. However, the ego is not meant to be the supreme ruler of our life. The true center of our life is the inner self or person dwelling in the depths of our unconscious being. When the ego is truly authentic, it will be the executive officer of the inner self, carrying out in our conscious life the will of God as discerned by the inner person. The ego is meant to be the servant of the self, which in turn is supposed to be united with and subservient to God.

We need a strong ego and strong will in order to fulfill the many tasks required for maturity. However, there is always the danger that the ego will attempt to become a law unto itself and rebel against humble submission to the voice of God speaking through the inner self. When this happens, we are guilty of egocentricity or pride.

A lifetime of self-discipline is required in order to maintain a proper relationship between the ego and the self. If we are successful, the ego will carry out the daily task of making contact with God through the voice of the inner self and then fulfill the tasks indicated by God. The ego is free to either obey or disobey God's will. (Another name for the voice of the inner self is the voice of conscience.) Through prayer, fasting, and reflection we form a right conscience which authentically reveals to our ego God's will. By listening to the voice of the inner self the ego attains authenticity and maturity.

Significance

Each of us has been given a significant part to play in the overall plan of God's creation. We need to discover our special destiny and purpose. A failure to find this by mid-life will often result in some sort of physical ailment or mental illness. However, if we discern our true significance in God's work on earth, our life becomes filled with energy and enthusiasm. Since our tasks on earth frequently change in the course of our life, we need to maintain a constant openness to God through prayer in order to know God's will for us each day. The whole work of creation might be compared to a giant symphony orchestra in which each of us has been assigned a special instrument and an individual musical score. Our task is to learn to play the melody assigned to us so that we make our contribution to the worldwide symphony of praise to God our Creator.

Transparency

We need to have a transparent personality and open heart in order to go out in love to every person we encounter. This means that we run the risk of being deeply wounded by those who take unfair advantage of our openness and transparency. Rather than being set back by this, we must try to continue to go out in love to all our fellow human beings. Our big concern will be that we use our life and our energies where we judge the most good will be accomplished. This transparency may even require the supreme sacrifice of laying down our life for others. "Greater love than this no one can have" (Jn 15:13). St. Paul speaks of this heroic love, "I will gladly spend myself and be spent for your sakes, even though loving you the more, I be loved the less" (II Cor 12:15). Only a very mature, unselfish person is capable of this kind of love.

Solidarity

Full maturity is attained only when we have learned to relate in a loving way to the various communities of which we are a part. Solidarity means to have a sense of oneness with the whole human race, so that we truly love all other human beings not only as individuals but as members of the different groups to which they belong, without racist, ethnic, or national bias. A sense of solidarity is attained by a realization of our creatureliness and our dependence upon God and one another. "No man is an island," a line from John Donne's poem of the same name, expresses humanity's universal connectedness. The experience of situations of need and help bring about this sense of oneness with others. It will occur when we are in need of help from others as well as when we go to the aid of others in need of our help.

The four tasks of individuation require our attention throughout our life on earth. However, there is a certain progress from one to the other. Without authenticity, we are unable to experience significance. Without a realization of our significance in God's plan of creation, it is very difficult to be transparent in love to other individuals. Without transparency, we will not attain solidarity. Together, the accomplishment of these four tasks will allow us to make a substantial contribution to the betterment of the world.

REFLECTION AND DISCUSSION

1. How is fear, whether of God, the world, others, or myself, holding me back from growing spiritually or psychologically? Decide on one step to take forward, to break through the fear and continue moving toward wholeness.

2. Consider the four steps of individuation: authenticity, significance, transparency, and solidarity. Where on your continuum of personal growth in these qualities do you identify yourself presently? What steps forward does this moment of reflection open to you?

CHAPTER 11

The Grace-Life of Supernatural Love

In this book we understand the supernatural as synonymous with grace. Some authors object to the distinction between nature and grace, insisting that everything is a grace from God. From one point of view this is quite true. However, our use of the word "supernatural" is to emphasize that God has gone far beyond what is necessary in order to save us. Besides all the natural gifts, which belong to our human nature in justice, God's infinite love has been extended far beyond anything justice might require. It is these extra gifts of love that we call supernatural graces. The supernatural life of grace is sharing in the same divine life that is shared by the three persons of the Blessed Trinity.

There are many points of similarity between nature and grace. It will help us to take the four elements of natural love and see how beautifully they apply to God's love for us through sanctifying grace. Strange as it may seem, God is fascinated by us and deeply concerned about each of us. God wants to reveal His/Her whole nature to us and desires to do everything possible to make us happy. Most of all S/He wills to be united with us forever through this grace-life by which we share the same intimate life as do the divine Father/Mother, Son and Holy Spirit. For God, life and love are interchangeable: to share in God's life means to be loved by God with all the fullness of divine being. "I have come that you may have life and have it more abundantly" (Jn 10:10).

In order to become partakers of the divine nature (II Pt 1:4), it is necessary that we freely choose to make a return of love to God in the same measure with which God has first loved us. We must allow ourselves to become involved in a tremendous fascination and attraction for God. Not only must we desire to know all we possibly can about God, we must also try to open ourselves completely to Him/Her so that we keep no secrets hidden. Third, our love of benevolence toward God will express itself by a constant desire to please God, to do God's will and obey His/Her commands. Finally, we should want more than anything else in the whole world to be united forever in love with our heavenly Father/Mother, with Jesus Christ, and with the Holy Spirit.

It should be quite evident that our weak, human nature could never alone accomplish the gigantic tasks expected of us when we love God with a supernatural love. We need special help from God and this comes to us in what is called actual or helping grace. God not only loves us in an infinite, supernatural way, God gives us the power to love Him/Her as S/He loves us. If we fail to make a proper response of love to God's call of grace, we can blame only ourselves. Since no love, natural or supernatural, can ever be forced, God will never compel us, against our will, to make a return of love. The grace-life of God's love is made available to us, and God lets us know in many ways how much S/He desires to share this life with us. God gives all the helping graces we need to make a return of love on a transcendental level. God then waits our response.

From the very beginning, God has called us to this life of grace. In a symbolic way the Book of Genesis speaks of God walking in the garden with Adam in the cool of the evening (Gn 3:8). This exemplifies the great intimacy that God wishes to have with us. Unfortunately we of the human race have decided again and again to reject God's offer of love. We try to find our satisfaction apart from God. However, God's love for us is so great that God continues to invite us to this life of grace. Down through the ages there were some who generously responded to God's call: Noah, Abraham, Moses, Samuel, Elijah, Isaiah, Daniel, and John the Baptist. There was one creature who better than any other answered God's loving call of grace. This was the Blessed Virgin Mary at the Annunciation. It was God's choice that through the child born of this woman, the whole of humankind would be given an opportunity to be united in love with the Blessed Trinity. It is through the incarnation of Jesus that we today are able to participate in the divine life of grace. Just as the power of God's Spirit lifted up the flesh of Mary and united it to God, so this same Holy Spirit, through grace-life, lifts up our body and soul into a supernatural union with God. We call this our "incarnation."

The law of incarnation will continue its work of uniting God and us through love until the whole of humankind has attained that union with divinity for which it has been destined. By joining ourselves to Jesus Christ through sanctifying grace, we fulfill this desire for unity with God. The Bible makes clear to what extremes God is willing to go to attain and maintain this love-union with us. On the other hand, the history of human race gives abundant illustration of the desire of humanity to partake of divinity. As St. Augustine states in his *Confessions*, "Our hearts are made for you, O God, and they shall not rest until they rest in you." When this ambition is misdirected, it becomes the sin of pride. If we are wise, we will know that it is only in submitting ourselves to God's will that we are able to fulfill this basic desire of ours to be like God. What we cannot do alone through nature is accomplished through grace.

Through sanctifying grace, we experience an incarnation that enables us to participate in the same three relationships of love that exist between the three Persons of the Blessed Trinity. God the heavenly Parent becomes our heavenly Mother/Father and we the adopted children in the family of God. God the Son becomes our divine Brother and we are united to him in the most intimate bonds of friendship. God, the Holy Spirit, is now our divine Partner through a spiritual union that is considerably more real and meaningful than any marriage union on earth. By means of grace-life the inner depths of our being are touched by the three Divine Persons and our whole nature is transformed. When we are living in grace it is as though a dead electric wire was connected to a giant dynamo, and our whole being is filled with the infinite energy, power and beauty of God's life. As far as God is concerned S/He desires that this union with us be permanent. S/He has promised to give us all the helping graces we need to keep us growing in each of the three loving relationships with the Divine Persons. If we cooperate with God's graces, we will experience a new incarnation each time a new contact with God is made, so that there is no limit to the heights of love that are available to us. It depends upon our decision when confronted with the grace of God.

Crisis in Knowledge of God

The interchange of supernatural love between God and ourselves will be filled with crises and struggles similar to those found in natural relationships of love. Because God is so infinite and different from creatures, it is difficult for us to know God as God really is. Indeed, even the words of our languages break down when we try to describe God's nature. Because God wants so much to reveal Him/Herself to us, divine ingenuity has devised many ways to allow us to know Him/Her. The best of these ways is the Incarnation of the God-Man. In Jesus Christ we are able to study God in human form. "He who sees me, sees also the Father" (Jn 14:9). We must allow ourselves to become intrigued with the divine personality of Jesus. If we make the effort to study the life of Christ, we can become so attracted to him that we will want to know everything about him. In the process of getting to know Jesus, we will encounter a number of facets in his personality that will be difficult to accept in all their literal fullness. For example Jesus' insistence on the value of poverty and the danger of riches goes counter to our whole American culture. Because they conflict with our own selfish desires, we will be tempted to reject them or water down their impact. The decisions that we make during these struggles with Christ and our conscience will determine the future course of our relationship of love with Christ and God.

Crisis in Revelation of Ourselves

Other crises develop during the growth of grace-life when we try to be completely open and honest with God. It is often anything but pleasant to admit before

God our deep egotism and other faults. We are tempted to make excuses for our behavior—trying to blame others, even God, for the way we have acted. We are ashamed to confess our deliberate betrayals of God's love. Since this is the price for growth in divine love, we may choose not to pay it. If so, our relationship with God becomes strained. There is danger that we may reject God's love rather than endure the agony of facing Him/Her with the full truth about ourselves.

Crisis in Benevolence Toward God

A third area of crisis in the progress of divine love is the question of how far we are willing to go in order to please God and do God's will. If we are to love God as S/He loves us, it is necessary that we make an all-out commitment in our efforts to do God's will. Again and again there will arise a conflict between what God wants and what we want. In each of these situations we must make a decision as to whether we will love God more than we love ourselves. The growth or decay of our grace-life is determined by our generosity or lack of generosity in doing God's will. God's helping grace will always be available, but ultimately, our own free choice will be the deciding factor in this whole relationship of supernatural love.

Crisis in Union with God

Every form of love has as its goal to be united with the beloved. In no relationship of natural love is this need of union as great as it is in the supernatural relationship of grace. God created the human race in order to unite us to Him/Herself in the closest possible bonds of love. God's desire for union is so great that S/He has persistently created new opportunities for us to be united in love with our Creator. For our part, we have been almost as persistent in rejecting the divine offers of love.

Much of the history of the human race is a tug-of-war between our waywardness and God's loving kindness in recalling us to the tasks of love. With the Incarnation, God won the most decisive of all battles in this struggle. In Jesus Christ, we have an everlasting marriage of the divine and human natures. In the God-Man, we have the first piece of that united Kingdom of heaven and earth which from all eternity God has desired. Never again will it be possible to separate the human race entirely from God. The Incarnation once started will never end. What took place in the womb of Mary at the Annunciation continues to happen each time we open our souls to the reception of grace. This grace-life encounters much resistance from those whom it seeks to incarnate into the divine level of supernatural love. But we have God's assurance in Sacred Scripture that the forward progress of the work of Incarnation will never cease. By our refusal to make a return of love to God, we hinder and delay the final day of victory. However, never will it be possible for us to destroy God's plan of a permanent union of love between us. One day, the Last Day, the work of Incarnation will come to an end, because on that day, the greatest of all days, God and all God's beloved people will be united forever.

REFLECTION AND DISCUSSION

1. As an individual, are you able to be completely transparent with your friends? With God? If not, what gets in the way? What difference does it make to know that God unconditionally loves you, even in sin and inadequacy?

2. With a friend, share ideas on what aids a growing intimacy with God. Share how God has given you the grace to do hard things in the past. How did you begin?

CHAPTER 12

The Sacraments as Sources of Grace-Life

From all eternity God has desired to share the divine life of love with us. During the long period of history before the coming of Jesus, God again and again made efforts to lift up our humanity to a supernatural life. Noah, Abraham and Moses responded to God's call of love. Each time this happened, God entered into a covenant of love with them and their descendants. These testaments of friendship required certain promises of love on the part of both God and us. God promised to make us His/Her own people in a very special way. We promised a return of love by being faithful children of God. As long as we were loyal to our promises, the covenant persevered and grew. Unfortunately the descendants of Abraham often broke the covenant of love by giving their service to false gods.

Some two thousand years ago, God chose to make a new and permanent covenant of love with the human race. This New Testament would be everlasting because it was made between God and Jesus Christ, the God-Man. With the coming of Jesus, the final age of this world began. The Kingdom of God upon earth was now established forever, and humanity had a most worthy representative who could make an adequate return of love to God. It was God's desire that all of us should join ourselves to Jesus by grace and through Christ make our return of love to God. Each outpouring of grace results in a new incarnation whereby our human nature is lifted up and united to God. This is accomplished in the same way that the first Incarnation took place—by a touching of God's person to our person. "The Holy Spirit shall come upon you and the power of the Most High shall overshadow you. Therefore, the Holy One to be born of you shall be called the Son of God" (Lk 1:35).

During his earthly life, Jesus usually bestowed his healing grace through contact with his physical body. Frequently our Lord would touch the person; at other times he would use the power of his Word to lift up a human being to union with God. These priestly actions of Jesus resulted in the sanctification of the whole person through a bestowal of grace-life. The touch of Jesus brought health and life to both body and soul. It was a continuation of the work of Incarnation whereby many other persons were lifted up and made members of God's family along with Christ, the first-born. Through contact with Jesus, they were able to participate in that wonderful exchange of love that flows between the three persons of the Holy Trinity. Salvation had come to them through contact with Jesus.

Before Christ ascended into heaven, he gave to the Church the power to carry on this same work of salvation. "As the Father has sent me, I also send you" (Jn 20:21). "He that hears you, hears me" (Lk 10:16). Just as an earthly spouse might be given the "power of attorney" by her husband before leaving on a long journey, so the Church received from Jesus the power to perform the same priestly actions as Christ when he was visibly on earth. It is through contact with the Church that we especially encounter Christ today. Whenever we are touched by Christ living in the Church, we experience a new incarnation; our whole being is lifted up by grace and united in bonds of supernatural love to God. "Whose sins you shall forgive, they are forgiven them" (Jn 20:21).

The priestly actions of the Church are called *sacraments*. Through them the work of incarnation will continue until Christ again returns visibly to earth on the Last Day. The sacraments retain their power and effectiveness only during this present "between-time," between the resurrection of Jesus and the final coming of Christ. In this present age of the world, Christ touches and sanctifies us through the outward signs of the sacraments. Each sacramental touch of Christ's church today possesses the same unlimited power to elevate us to the divine level of grace as did the actions of Jesus Christ during his public life. The effect of each worthy reception of a sacrament extends far beyond our own individual soul. The entire family of God's people benefits from each new infusion of grace into our person. Our whole being, body and soul, is healed of the wounds of sin and prepared for the day when Christ will establish his Kingdom in all its fullness. The graces of the sacraments gradually release us from the slavery we now experience in the areas of fear, pain, confusion, ignorance, self-indulgence and death.

We will limit our discussion to the four sacraments that many Christians have in common: Baptism, Confirmation, Reconciliation and Eucharist. If we will make proper use of these sacraments, we will be able to grow constantly in the life of grace, preparing ourselves for the perfect union of love with God, which Christ wants to share with us. Each of these sacraments fulfills a special need in our lives, providing us not only with sanctifying grace but also becoming a ready source of actual grace needed for our growth and perseverance. Two of them, baptism and confirmation, are permanent sacraments in the sense that once received, their power to bestow grace is always ready to go to work during the rest of our life on earth, provided we fulfill the proper dispositions. All of the sacraments give grace in proportion to the dispositions of faith, hope and charity, which we bring to them. Each sacrament is filled with the infinite power of God and there is no limit to the degree of union with God which we are capable of attaining, provided we cooperate by opening our whole being in generous, unselfish love.

The Sacrament of Baptism

Through baptism our whole nature is consecrated to God in a permanent way. The indelible character of baptism works a radical transformation of our whole being and unites us to Christ in such a way that we are made members of his Body and share in all the mysteries of his life: birth, death, resurrection and ascension. This sacrament acts like a giant press which squeezes our whole nature into the mold of Christ. We are thus permanently transformed to the very depths of our being into the likeness of Christ. Just as the flesh in Mary's womb was touched by the Holy Spirit and was irrevocably transformed into the God-Man, so baptism makes over our whole human nature into new sons and daughters of God, other Christs.

Once received, the graces of baptism are available to us any moment of the day or night. As long as we remain on earth, we need only to renew and intensify our faith commitment to God and Jesus Christ and the giant motors of grace-life, bestowed at baptism, start humming within the depths of our soul. The more generous and sincere is the commitment of our faith, the more intensely we will be united with God through the grace-life that flows from this sacrament. Frequently, the graces of baptism lie dormant in our souls, like seeds in the cold, winter soil. Regardless of how long they have lain fallow in our hearts, we need only to apply the proper moisture of the tears of conversion, the necessary light of God's truth and the warmth of a generous love for God. Immediately the seeds of grace that were first sown at baptism will spring up into a luscious new growth of supernatural life in our souls.

The Sacrament of Confirmation

By baptism we are born into the family of God; through confirmation we reach a certain supernatural maturity. Our confirmation in many ways resembles the turning point in the life of Jesus, which took place at his baptism in the River Jordan. This was the end of his hidden life and the beginning of his public life of service to the community of God's people. At his baptism, the heavenly Father gave Jesus the commission to go out and redeem the world. The Holy Spirit came down upon Jesus to strengthen him for the tremendous mission assigned by the Father. The same thing happens to us when we receive confirmation. No longer are we allowed to lead the hidden life of a private citizen in the family of God. The bishop, as the representative of the heavenly Father, commissions us to go out and be a good minister for Christ, struggling to establish the Kingdom of God throughout the world. The Holy Spirit touches our person and consecrates us to the apostolate of bringing others into the fold of Christ and helping those who are already there to become more perfect. The very word *confirmation* means that this sacrament confirms and strengthens us for the particular ministry assigned to us in the family of God.

Through the character of confirmation we are once again pressed into the mold of Christ and given a permanent share in his priestly ministry. The graces of this sacrament are always available to us, provided we use the right key to release them. The key that unlocks the graces of confirmation is a generous charity towards Christ and our brothers and sisters. As long as we are willing to devote all the energies of our being to the work of the ministry, immense graces are released through the permanent presence of the Holy Spirit within our souls. As Christians, we have been commissioned by Christ to assist him in the priestly tasks of teaching, guiding and sanctifying other persons. If we cooperate with the powers of confirmation, every possible grace we need will be given us.

The Sacrament of Reconciliation

A third sacrament which is available to all Christians is that of reconciliation or penance. It is Christ's Easter gift, the profound outcome of His Pascal sacrifice, bestowed upon us as a sacrament of peace, joy and mercy. Penance is a real touch of Christ's healing hand to our wounded souls and bodies. Just as Jesus healed the sinners and the suffering of Galilee two thousand years ago, so our wounded natures are healed through the sacrament of reconciliation today. In no sacrament does so much depend upon our preparation for its reception as does penance. This sacrament has been called "laborious baptism" because much effort is required on our part to have our sins taken away. Routine, mechanical confession without any real conversion of the heart, is not only a waste of time, it is a real insult to the merciful love of our Savior. Before we go to reconciliation we must make the effort to turn away from all attachment to sin and turn back to God with our whole heart and soul. We call this conversion "metanoia". As was explained in the chapter on *"Growth in Wholeness and Maturity,"* we need to experience many conversions in our progress towards maturity and sanctity. Each reception of the sacrament of penance provides us with the wonderful opportunity to reject sin and all false love and dedicate our energies to a proper love of God, others and self. This sacramental metanoia requires a real humiliation on our part and often is quite difficult. We must acknowledge God's authority over us and God's right to lead us as S/He might see fit. We must accept our need of begging for mercy from God, realizing that in strict justice we have no absolute right to forgiveness. Relying on God's infinite goodness and promises, we hope to obtain pardon and we humbly ask for it, promising that we will go to any extreme to avoid sin in the future. All of this is necessary in order to possess the proper spirit of penance for a fruitful reception of this sacrament.

We can never be grateful enough for this wonderful sacrament. Without its encouragement, most of us would postpone or neglect entirely the effort necessary to have a proper metanoia. The most difficult part in the whole work of natural and supernatural perfection is the effort required to endure successfully the many conversions of heart needed by us. If we will take seriously our preparation for penance and not be content with a routine examination of conscience and a mechanical confession, then each reception of this sacrament will be a giant step toward maturity and sanctity. As far as possible, we should make each preparation for the sacrament of penance a turning point in our lives. We should try to face boldly the unpleasant truth of one or more of our evil tendencies. If we are honest with ourselves, we will discover many imperfect and shameful attitudes lurking in the depths of our soul. We regress from maturity and sanctity if we ignore them. Whether we recognize these wayward tendencies in ourselves or not, damage is done unless we honestly do all in our power to transform them into virtues. The graces of the sacrament of penance enable us to do just that—to convert our evil into good.

The Sacrament of the Eucharist

There is a fourth sacrament that all Christians have in common: the Eucharist. Above all else, it is the great bond of unity between God and us and between one Christian and another during this period of the second aeon. We can never say enough about the Eucharist, so we will return to its consideration again and again in future chapters. It is the sacrament that we receive more often than all the others combined. It completes the work of grace that was begun in the sacrament of Baptism and continued through confirmation and penance. Ordinarily it should be the sacrament we receive before dying, under the form of Holy Viaticum—food for the journey from this life of grace to life with God in heaven. We call it the "blessed sacrament" because it is the glorified body of Christ and, therefore, the most precious and most holy of all the sacraments.

It is important that we center the Eucharist in the divine Father/Mother rather than just in the Son, Jesus Christ. The sacramental Christ of the Eucharist is God's gift to us to help us go to God. It is given us to nourish the grace-life received at baptism. Through the Eucharist, our love for God should grow with each reception. It is a continual expression of the love of God for us and our love for God. During the Eucharistic service we should make use of the Eucharist to express the gift of ourselves through Christ to God the Father/Mother. We should receive it in Holy Communion as God's gift, expressing the divine acceptance of our gifts and God's good pleasure with us and His/Her great love for us. The Eucharistic Banquet is a love-feast, an agape meal where all of God's friends should experience a loving encounter with each other as well as with God. The sacrament of the Eucharist was never meant to be a mere private union with God to the exclusion of our brothers and sisters. Never should we be so conscious of the family of God as when united with Jesus in the Eucharist. Instead of considering those around us a distraction, we should desire after receiving the Eucharist to join them in joyous songs of praise and thanksgiving.

Each Eucharist, along with baptism, confirmation and penance, adds to our capacity to know, love and serve God and our brothers and sisters. However, the tremendous powers contained in these sacraments will not operate unless we open our hearts in loving response to

God's calls of grace. The sacraments unfold their effectiveness in proportion to the dispositions of the recipient. The main dispositions required of us are faith, hope and charity. The more generously we respond to each sacrament by believing, hoping and loving, the more progress will be made towards wholeness and perfection of our being, both naturally and supernaturally. These virtues are actually three steps of love which we are able to make in reply to God's invitation to love. Unaided nature would find it impossible to make a single act of faith, hope or charity. On the other hand, grace without the aid of nature is also helpless in eliciting these virtues in us. Only a union of God's grace and our cooperation enables us to form the dispositions needed to receive the sacraments profitably.

REFLECTION AND DISCUSSION

1. Four sacraments are the focus of consideration in this chapter: baptism, confirmation, reconciliation, and Eucharist. Consider an event or time during which one of these had special significance for you. Recall that event or time in as much detail as you can. How can you apply the power of that encounter with God to present events?

2. These sacraments occur within the context of community. As participants in the spiritual community, how can we create an environment in which these sacraments are received in a more compelling way? Discuss what our contribution can be both as individuals and as community.

CHAPTER 13

Our Response of Faith to God's Call

The first and most necessary disposition for a fruitful reception of the sacraments is faith. Faith means the acceptance of God and God's will as the guiding light of our life. It entails a total, blind commitment of our will to the will of God. Faith is a new incarnation—a new union of God and humanity upon earth. As the first Incarnation was possible only when Mary freely consented to God's proposal, so faith is born only when we freely choose to respond generously to God's call of love. Every act of faith is the result of the free choice of both God and ourselves; one without the other is never able to give us faith. God's part in faith comes through helping grace, showered upon every person who comes into this world. St. Paul assures us that God wishes "all men to be saved and to come to the knowledge of the truth" (I Tim 2:4).

These helping graces precede the reception of the sacraments and are even given to souls cut off from God by sin. They are like sparks of divine fire which God mercifully showers upon all humankind. If we will cherish these sparks and gently fan them with our efforts to love, they will grow into a blazing fire of supernatural faith. Each reception of a sacrament intensifies both the sparks and our capacity for holding this fire. The Holy Spirit pours out the fires of grace upon every soul willing to receive them. The more generously we respond to grace, the brighter and more intense will faith and love burn in our souls. The more filled we are with the light and heat of faith and love, the more we will warm all our neighbors who surround us. The nearer they come to us, the more they will be enlightened by our faith and love. God's helping grace comes to us not only directly but also indirectly through the community of our brothers and sisters. Anyone on fire with faith, hope and charity is like a highly charged transformer throwing off sparks of grace, and we need only draw near to be influenced by our contact.

Faith in its fullness is primarily an experience of love which can never be explained through words. We need actually to taste it ourselves before we are able to know what people mean when they talk about faith. Faith adds a new dimension to reality; by it we step into a whole new world, the supernatural world of God. Faith is like a breach in the wall that now separates us from God's world. It is the gate that opens into heaven and connects us with the things of eternity. On the Last Day, we will see God face to face, but now during the second aeon we must simply accept all these wonderful things of God on faith. We are like blind persons who are forced to "see" through feeling. If we open our hearts generously to the graces of faith, we will begin to feel and experience the realities of God so vividly that it will be almost like seeing them.

Faith begins as a little mustard seed, a tender little plant or a newborn babe. It must be carefully nurtured, especially at first. We must protect it from the cold winds of doubt, from the flames of passion, from the contamination of worldly, faithless companions. We must water it with the tears of our contrition and warm it with the heat of a generous love. It needs the bright sunlight of God's truth as found in the Bible and the traditions of the Church. Its growth will be aided greatly by the presence of other persons who are filled with strong faith, high hopes and generous love. It grows best in the bosom of the family of God's holy people and during the beautiful experience of a fine liturgical service. Any increase in our intimacy with Jesus Christ will foster a proportionate increase in our faith.

Supernatural faith grows in proportion to our growth in natural maturity. Since faith is a mature encounter of love with God's person, the more mature our own person is, the easier it should be to respond to this call of grace. As we grow in maturity, we grow in the freedom and ability to make decisions for ourselves. Since faith is making a decision for Christ and for God's plans in our regard, natural wholeness enables us to make a stronger commitment to God. It takes great courage to close our eyes, put our hand into the hand of God and say, "Yes, heavenly Father, I accept your will for me. Lead on. Take me wherever you wish—even to Calvary and death upon a cross." The courage needed for the commitment of faith is both supernatural and natural. God's helping grace will provide the supernatural fortitude, and the more naturally mature and responsible we are, the easier it will be to cooperate with this grace. On the other hand, the more faith we have, the more quickly our nature will grow toward wholeness and maturity.

The challenge of faith should be in proportion to the degree of maturity and responsibility a person possesses. To demand too heroic a commitment from an immature person will do more harm than good. As one progresses through childhood and youth, a more and more generous response of faith should be asked. If the Eucharistic liturgy is celebrated properly for the various feasts of the year, ample opportunity will be given for the community of God's people to make their proper commitment to God. The climax each year will be the renewal of the baptismal vows during the Easter vigil service. If the necessary effort is made during Lent to have a good metanoia, everyone in the congregation will be ready to increase one's faith on Holy Saturday night according to the particular stage of one's maturity. Very special and abundant helping grace from God will be available to all taking part in the service. The presence of mature and heroically generous souls among the community will help the less courageous and less generous to rise to the occasion. The whole service should bring a beautiful personal and community experience of faith to everyone who is present.

From a natural point of view, every experience of love with other human beings will be a tremendous boost to our powers of faith. The more personal is the atmosphere of the home, the parish and the community the easier it will be for everyone present to make the commitment of faith that God asks of us. Natural love should not be considered an enemy to faith, but rather one of its most important allies. Without good experiences of human love, it will be extremely difficult for anyone to make the heroic acts of faith needed for sanctity. The more selfless is this love we receive and give to one another, the greater our ability to make the blind commitment to God which we call faith.

Faith and trust in another human being follow love rather than precede it. There comes a moment in the life of two lovers when one makes a proposal of permanent union between them. If the proposal is to be accepted an act of natural faith must be made. Just as in earthly love, by faith we put our hand in the hand of God and say, "Yes, I accept your proposal. I am willing to trust myself completely to you. I do not know what the future holds, but I love you enough to surrender my whole life into your hands. I give you permission to do anything you want with me. I no longer choose to lead my own, selfish life. I want to live your life, to share everything you have; to see things as you see them; to love others as you love them; to live as you live. I commit my future destiny completely to you."

At baptism the first response of faith is made to God. Just as a man and woman exchange their vows of marriage, just as God and the people of God exchanged their promises of love at Mount Sinai, so the baptismal promises are the exchange of vows between God and ourselves at the beginning of our life of faith. Most of us little realize what we are promising when first baptized. However, God asks only a response that is proportionate to our ability at the time. As we mature, our commitment to God should become more and more generous. Each time we renew our baptismal vows, God's helping grace will enable us to take another step toward the total incarnation of our being with that of God. If we do our part in the growth toward natural and supernatural wholeness, the rate of our increase in faith will become considerably swifter as the years of life progress. Our first mature commitment of faith should take place around the age of fifteen to twenty. By the time we are forty years of age we should be experiencing a tremendous increase of faith every year. If we are unaware of any growth in our faith, year after year, we should give serious consideration to the situation of our life. It does not necessarily mean something is wrong, but the presumption is that somewhere we need to make some changes. It would be wise not to depend merely upon our own judgment in such a serious matter of faith. An experienced spiritual director should be able to diagnose the problem and suggest suitable remedies.

Because faith is a participation in the incarnation of Christ, it brings about profound changes in our whole being. Our intellects are given new powers to understand so that we have insights into the mysteries of God. The voice of our conscience becomes the voice of God, revealing to us God's secret desires, counseling us what to say and do at any given time. We are able to recognize the hand of God in the events of our own life and perhaps in the lives of others. We are given the power to judge according to God's standards and to make the right decisions in accord with God's will for us. Those who live the life of faith live in a new world—the world of grace. Having committed ourselves into the hands of God, everything will appear differently from what it did when we judged things purely from an earthly point of view. It is like receiving a supernatural Extra Sensory Perception. We see things we never saw in the past, although we may have been looking at these same things all of our lives. By faith we attain a new and higher standpoint from which to judge reality.

Standing on the outside looking in, the world of faith is filled with darkness. The first steps of faith are usually carried out in total blindness as we surrender ourselves to God without knowing what is ahead of us. However, as we progress in faith, we begin to realize that the really blind people are those outside the realm of divine faith. Sin darkens our intellects so that without faith, we wander about the world like blind persons. Like Bartimeus, we hear the noise of a crowd passing and we inquire what this may be. "And they told him that Jesus of Nazareth was passing by. And he cried out, saying, 'Jesus, Son of David, have mercy on me.' Jesus asked him, 'What would you have me do for you?' And he said, 'Lord, that I may see.' And Jesus said to him, 'Receive your sight, your faith has saved you'" (Lk 18:37-42).

Jesus Christ is present in the Church today. In each sacrament we receive, Jesus of Nazareth passes by. If we have the same desire to see that the blind beggar Bartimeus had, Jesus will touch us in the sacrament and we will begin to see everything through the eyes of Christ. It is not enough to make just one act of faith. Since faith is capable of unlimited increase, we can renew our faith each time we receive a sacrament and especially during the Eucharist each Sunday. We should prepare for the commitment we make during the Liturgy by studying the beautiful examples of faith given us in the Sacred Scriptures. With Samuel we should say many times each day, "Speak, Lord, your servant is listening" (I Sam 3:10). With Isaiah we should offer ourselves generously to the work of God as we arise each morning, "Here I am, send me" (Is 6:8). With the Blessed Virgin Mary at the Incarnation, let us keep our hearts and souls constantly open to God's grace and commit our whole being to the doing of God's will, "Behold the handmaid of the Lord, be it done to me according to your word" (Lk 1:38).

In the third aeon we will no longer have any need of faith since we will see God face to face. In the New Jerusalem the streets will be paved with the pure gold of divine love (Rev 21:21). But as long as we remain in our present condition, faith and hope are essential to any relationship of love with God. They form the necessary foundation for charity and together these three virtues comprise the response of love which we give to God's call of grace. Both the individual and the whole community of God's people must make these commitments. They should be especially made when we are united to our brothers and sisters of the believing community during each liturgical celebration. Again and again during the different feasts of the liturgical year, we should join ourselves to Christ in offering to the heavenly Mother/Father God a perfect service of faith, hope and charity.

REFLECTION AND DISCUSSION

1. "Faith means the acceptance of God and God's will as the guiding light of our lives. It entails a total, blind commitment of our will to the will of God." What are some of the issues in your life that impede your abandonment to God's will? What are you prepared to do to place yourself in a place of greater acceptance?

2. Revisit your baptismal promises, and reflect upon their power to renew your life.

CHAPTER 14

Finding Hope Through the Liturgy

What would we do without hope? It is hope that fills us with enthusiasm for the future and helps us to overcome present difficulties. Hope brings joy, peace, confidence and courage as we struggle with our day-to-day problems. By giving us a goal both attainable and attractive, hope furnishes the motivation to keep us moving forward. Those who are filled with hope for the future remain young in spirit, open to new ideas and are possessed of an elasticity that enables them to keep growing in perfection. Without hope, our whole life becomes gloomy and sterile. We are filled with discouragement and lack energy to do anything about it. When hope is lacking, fear and cowardice take possession of a person.

Christian hope is the supernatural incarnation of natural courage. By means of God's grace, a person of faith is able to make this second response of love to God's call. The virtue of hope is totally dependent upon a previous commitment of faith. Having taken this first step of faith, we need hope to keep us going. Through hope we are able to transcend time and live by anticipation in the future Kingdom of God. It is especially during our participation in the liturgy of the Church that we enter at least for a moment into the life of the third aeon. The glorified body of Christ that we receive in the Eucharist is a substantial piece of this future Kingdom now present in the second aeon. This liturgical preview of coming attractions is experienced under the veil of faith; therefore, it is considerably less than the face-to-face vision of God after death or the direct experiences of the Last Day. Nevertheless, the liturgical worship of the Christian community is a real anticipation of life in the New Jerusalem. The degree of our realization of this will be in proportion to our faith.

The Church today stands on the border that separates the second from the third aeon. During the liturgy we are able to make contact with the glorified Body of Christ. In the Liturgy of the Word, the glorified Christ speaks to us through the Scripture lessons and the homily. We are able to speak directly to God and offer the gift of ourselves through Christ. In the Eucharist we are nourished with the body of the resurrected Christ. By means of the Eucharistic symbols we are able to experience something of the splendor, glory and beauty of Christ's Kingdom of the Last Day. During the course of the Liturgical Year not only do we relive the events of the life of Jesus in Galilee and Jerusalem, but we anticipate the life of the whole Body of Christ forever in the New Jerusalem.

During the liturgy, our goal of the third aeon becomes present. If we have the faith to accept this, the Eucharist and the Sacraments become for us tremendous sources of courage and strength. If the liturgy is properly celebrated by celebrant and people, those present will receive special graces to overcome discouragement. First of all, we will become keenly aware of our union with the rest of the community of God's people. We will realize that we do not have to fight the battles of life alone, but we have many sisters and brothers to help us.

We will also have an experience of a personal encounter with Jesus Christ during the high points of the liturgical service. Christ will come to us and join forces with us in the battles of life. We will be lifted up by the Holy Spirit as a result of our participation in the liturgy and will benefit from a generous outpouring of the gifts of the Spirit. When we leave the liturgical worship, we will carry with us a profound conviction that we have at last been able to satisfy the infinite debt of love and worship that we owe to God. Through Christ and in union with the Holy Spirit and our sisters and brothers we will have offered a perfect gift to God.

None of these wonderful things are accomplished without effort on our part. Many things are required to make a fine liturgical celebration. It helps if our bodies and minds are well rested and alert, capable of living for a time on the high personal level required during liturgical worship. However, grace and the enthusiasm of the community can often overcome our physical lethargy. Both priest and people need to be well prepared intellectually and psychologically through study and meditation on the mysteries about to be celebrated. The actual service needs to be carried out in a sincere, reverent and meaningful way so that the words, actions and symbols are readily understandable to all. The celebrant and people need to be sufficiently familiar with the mechanics of the service so that these do not become a distraction to them, but rather the instrument to make contact with the glorified life of Jesus. Each person should be ready to make a total commitment of oneself in faith and love to the Father through Christ and in union with the Holy Spirit.

It should be the aim of everyone in the community of worshipers to make the liturgy a communal endeavor. Individuals should sacrifice their own personal desires about the way they like to pray during the service. All should join together in singing and praying, according to the particular functions of each member of the group. Everyone should be conscious of the fact that the whole liturgical service is a community work, from the beginning to the end. Sacrificing personal tastes, we should aim to make it a community experience of union with Christ.

Every covenant of love that God has made with the human race has been a community covenant. The Old Testament was made with Abraham and his descendants. In all these pacts of love, God has insisted that the whole community of the people should renew the covenant with God on certain occasions set by God himself. In the Old Testament there were certain festival days each year when the people of God gathered around the Ark of the Covenant or in the temple and renewed their promises to God. On the Sabbath smaller groups of the family of God gathered in the synagogue for a further renewal of their covenant with God. In the New Testament, Christians are called upon to gather around the altar of the Lord at least once each week on the Lord's Day and there to renew their covenant of love with God. This is the primary reason for our assisting at Eucharist each Sunday. We come here at the command of Christ to renew our promises of love and faithfulness to God. We are expected to come as a community, the new family of God, the Church and the parish of which we are members. Together with our brothers and sisters we renew our covenant with God.

While at Mass we listen attentively to the reading and explanation of God's word. It is here that we find God's instructions for the coming days. Together we make known our needs and petitions to the Lord. We make a solemn offering of our faith, hope and love through Jesus to God. Christ takes our gifts, transforms them in the Eucharistic prayer and unites them to the gift of his own Body and Blood. Then together, Christ and the Faithful, united through the Holy Spirit, offer their gift of love, loyalty and commitment to God. Now it is God's turn to renew the covenant of love that was made with the human race at the Incarnation of Jesus on earth. It is a part of this covenant to assure us of God's faithfulness to all the promises made to the people of God. God promises to take care of us, to give us the grace we need to reach the Kingdom on the Last Day. As a visible sign of this love, God gives us the glorified Body of Christ in Holy Communion. God insists that we take this symbol of love and eat it, thus uniting us most intimately with God and Jesus.

Coming forth from our Sunday liturgy, we should be filled with the spirit of God. We need no longer be afraid of the world, ourselves, others. We should have the bold spirit of conquerors, ready to go forth and do battle with the forces of evil and overcome them. We are now ready to tackle the problems of life with renewed vigor. We should be filled with the highest hopes of victory, since we carry within us Jesus Christ the conqueror of sin, death and evil. There will be moments in our life when we feel tired and weak, when temptations threaten to overwhelm us. If we will only think back to last Sunday's Eucharist or forward to next Sunday's liturgy, we shall find the hope necessary to keep going ahead. For those fortunate enough to assist at daily Mass, there is even less reason for discouragement in the face of the difficulties of life. Throughout the day we carry within us the spirit of the triumphal Christ. Throughout the night we can look forward to a new encounter with the victorious Christ at the beginning of another new day.

The liturgy of the Eucharist should fill us with joy. There are times during the year when it is proper to emphasize the sufferings and death of Jesus. But even these Masses insist upon the joys of the resurrection that will soon follow. The whole Christian religion is one of triumph and victory, not of sadness and defeat. If the liturgy is celebrated as it should be, the people will come forth filled with joy and hope for the future. While at Mass we may be conscious of the fact that we are still pilgrims and exiles, making the long desert journey to the third aeon. We look forward with eager longing for the final coming of Christ. But we should never doubt the outcome since each Mass celebrates the victory over evil and death accomplished already by Jesus Christ.

Once we understand the purpose of the liturgy and participate in it fully, Christian hope will be an ever-present reality for us. The events of our redemption and salvation are made present and the future goal of God's Kingdom is anticipated. Through the power of this hope our fears are conquered and we go forward with joy and enthusiasm to whatever God has in store for us. Having made our commitment of faith, the virtue of hope keeps us going on the road with full speed ahead until we arrive at our destination of union with God. All the sacraments give us hope, but the Eucharist is its greatest source. In Jesus' promise regarding the Eucharist, it is the present tense of the verb that is used. "He who eats my flesh and drinks my blood *has* life everlasting and I will raise him up on the Last Day" (Jn 6:55).

REFLECTION AND DISCUSSION

1. Reflect on how the mass has been a source of hope for you. Were you ever surprised by hope at the Eucharistic liturgy, in spite of yourself? Describe that time. How might you allow yourself to be more open to the promise and joy of the Eucharist?

2. Think about what creates a good celebration of the mass. Consider all that happens before and during the liturgy to make this happen. Realizing that the celebration takes on the character of all the participants, whether or not they have a role of presentation, how can you enrich the celebration for other members of the congregation?

CHAPTER 15

Living with Christ Through the Liturgical Year

In his loving kindness, God has given us a most beautiful way to express our love for him in the second aeon. The liturgy of the Mass, as celebrated in the different feasts of the liturgical year, relives the whole history of salvation. By means of the historical dimension of the liturgy, the events of the past, especially the life of Christ, are made present as we celebrate Christmas, Epiphany, Holy Week, Easter and Ascension. "As often as you shall eat this bread and drink the cup, you proclaim the death of the Lord, until he comes" (I Cor 11:26). At the same time, the liturgy anticipates the events yet to come by means of the eschatological or future dimension. During Mass, time ceases to exist and we live for a while in the eternal "now" where the past, present and future are all one. We make contact with those events of long ago that brought us our salvation. At the same time, we live for a few moments in the third aeon, which we hope to attain on the Last Day. This life of the future is experienced behind the veil of faith, but nevertheless, it is an actual experience for those who have the grace.

The history of salvation, past and future, is experienced in two ways during the Liturgy of the Mass: through the Liturgy of the Word and the Liturgy of the Eucharist. In the Liturgy of the Word, our contact with the past and future is made through the words of Sacred Scripture.

During the Liturgy of the Eucharist, the symbols of the consecrated bread and wine are used to unite us to the living Christ, past, present and future. It is impossible for our limited minds and hearts to have a satisfactory experience with all these events within the confines of one Mass. Therefore, the Church has wisely stretched the celebration of the history of salvation over the course of the whole liturgical year. We have more time now to dwell on these great events, and we find a freshness and variety in our liturgical celebrations, which adds to our appreciation and enjoyment.

What we read and hear in Sacred Scripture tells us something of the actual events of past history. By means of grace-life, these events are made present. In addition, the Scripture contains a message concerning the future life in the Kingdom of God. What God did in the past indicates what he intends to do in the present and the future, but not in exactly the same way. The Christian interpretation of history is not a closed circle but a spiral movement that mounts ever higher and higher until it attains its goal in the third aeon. Again and again we come back to a similar situation, but always from a higher point of view. The words of Scripture describe this whole journey up the spiral ladder to the life of everlasting union with God. What is said in the Bible is applicable to life at any stage of growth from the beginning to the completion of the Kingdom on the Last Day. When in the domain of Scripture, time disappears and we consider things from the point of view of eternity.

What is true of the reading of Sacred Scripture in general is especially true when it is proclaimed at Mass during the Liturgy of the Word. All its dimensions come to life as we listen to the Word of God spoken and explained through the liturgy. In Advent, we are back with the prophets and other people of the Old Testament, longing for the coming of Christ. At the same time, we are preparing for his coming now in the Eucharist and later on the Last Day. Everything that Isaiah and the Baptist said to prepare the people for the first coming of Christ can be applied during the present Advent to our preparations for his coming in the Mass and for his final coming at the end of time. As we participate in Advent each year, we must try to keep all three dimensions in mind. To enjoy the full experience of liturgical living, we need the help of the whole community. Each member of the congregation is given a particular task to perform, and it is only when everyone cooperates that we attain the fullness of a liturgical celebration.

During the Easter cycle, we renew the events of our redemption as first experienced by Jesus Christ two thousand years ago. Through our devout participation in the liturgy of Holy Week and the Paschal Season, these events of the past are made present so that we can share in them. If we are in tune with the liturgy, we will experience a real death in our life of sin and evil attachments during Lent and Holy Week. During the great service of the Easter Vigil we will go through a personal resurrection of grace in the solemn proclamation of Christ's resurrection. We will also take part by anticipation in the future events of our own death and the glorious resurrection from the dead. These events happen to us through faith, but this does not mean that it is unreal. Only those can understand who have actually tasted the joy and happiness of an encounter with the living Christ during a liturgical celebration.

On the Feast of the Ascension, we commemorate the first Ascension of Christ into heaven and we celebrate our own ascension today by means of grace into the bosom of the heavenly Father; most of all, we anticipate the glorious ascension of the whole human race on the Last Day. Similarly, at Pentecost we renew the first Descent of the Holy Spirit, we participate in a new descent of the Spirit by means of grace, and we experience something of the encounter with the Holy Spirit that will take place on the Last Day.

Those who carry out liturgical services in the proper way will never envy the people of Christ's time, nor those who will still be alive on the Last Day. Through faith, they are able to share in the same joys and blessings as did the apostles on the first Easter and Pentecost and as will those who are alive at the final coming of Christ. There is always the veil of faith hiding from our eyes a direct vision of these events of liturgy, but as we grow in faith year by year, this blindness will mean less and less. There are other ways to experience an encounter of love with the living Christ. We should look forward with expectation to the beatific vision in heaven and the renewed creation of the Last Day; nevertheless, we can appreciate the special value of a life of faith and hope. During this present aeon we love God in a way that after death we will never again have the opportunity to do. While on earth, we are able to prove our love for God by loving him blindly through acts of faith. This heroism will no longer be possible in heaven or in the third aeon. If we value our present opportunities, we will make the most of them as long as God sees fit to leave us upon earth. Faith and hope are essential to an encounter with Christ during liturgy; on the other hand, the more real experience we have in liturgical living, the stronger will become our faith and hope.

During the liturgy of the Eucharist, we actually celebrate what has just been proclaimed and explained in the scripture lessons and homily. Through the symbols of bread and wine our life is united to the life of the Blessed Trinity; the Holy Spirit unites us to Christ and Christ presents us to the Father. The Father is pleased with the gifts which Christ presents to him and desires to show his joy by sharing with us the gift that is closest to his heart, the Body and Blood of his Son. At the banquet table of the Lord, we are privileged to partake of this food, and through the symbolism of eating we are united with Christ and through Christ with the Father, the Spirit, and all our brethren.

There is an infinite variety in the offering and eating of the Body and Blood of Christ. The Eucharist, which we celebrate and receive on Christmas, should be different from the one at Ascension or Pentecost. According to the spirit of each season and feast, we offer and receive Christ. In addition, the Eucharist is celebrated each year according to the disposition of the people who take part in it. The more we grow in grace, the more we can unite ourselves to Christ in the various events of his life. The better the whole community participates in the liturgical service, the greater will be their individual union with Christ. As the people of God in a particular parish come to understand the deeper meaning of the liturgy, the Eucharistic celebrations will become new and fresh experiences for everyone participating. We live in God's world and God's time during liturgy, and there is no end to the possibilities of encounter.

Those who lack faith see only the external symbols that conceal the internal grace. "Seeing, they may see but not perceive; and hearing, they may hear but not understand" (Mk 4:12). If the music, vestments and gestures are beautiful, those merely watching the spectacle may experience a certain elevation of their spirits. They might find themselves inspired by a beautiful liturgical ceremony, so that they can pray more reverently and fervently while the liturgy is being performed in their presence. However, this is only the shell or the rind; the real fruit of the liturgy is hidden from these people and is reserved for those who can participate in the service with an intelligent and genuine faith and hope. It is unfortunate that so many Christians lack the understanding and faith needed to experience the real encounters with Christ that are available in the liturgy.

The language of the liturgy is the language of love. Only those who have had satisfying experiences of love are able to enter into the full action of a liturgical celebration. The Church's liturgy is so rich that everyone can derive some benefit from it, provided he has good will. However, the more real love, both natural and supernatural, that exists in our hearts, the more capable we will be of entering into the intensity of union available to us at every Mass. Besides love, there is need of an appreciation of the meaning of the particular feast. This requires study or explanation as well as time for reflection. For many centuries, the Church has very wisely expected religious and other devout people to prepare for their participation in the liturgy by a period of meditation. On the Sundays and greater feasts, this preparation should begin the previous night by means of a Bible Service, either publicly or privately. For the greatest of all liturgical celebrations, the Easter Vigil Service, all of Lent and especially Holy Week are meant to be a preparation. Even our bodies need to be prepared for liturgy by the proper rest and relaxation so that we can give our whole selves to the encounter with Christ.

In the twenty-first chapter of St. John's gospel, there is a beautiful scene in the life of the apostles after the Resurrection of Christ. This scripture passage describes the experience of love that we should have at the beginning of each day as we celebrate the eucharistic liturgy. The apostles had spent the whole night on the lake without catching any fish. Early in the morning, weary and discouraged, they are rowing back to shore. A voice speaks to them across the water; "Have you any fish?" "No," they reply. "Cast the net to the right of the boat and you will find them." They cast, and were unable to draw it up for the great number of fish it contained. The disciple whom Jesus loved said, "It is the Lord!"

St. Gregory the Great, in his description of this gospel passage, tells us that Peter's boat represents the Church and the lake illustrates the ups and downs of life in this second aeon. In the darkness of the early morning, our blessed Lord directs our work in the apostolate from the shore of the third aeon. If we obey him, we will catch such a number of fish that the boat cannot contain them; but we will have to row to shore, dragging the net after us. There on the shore, in the dawn of a new day, stands our Lord. When, therefore, they had landed, they saw a fire ready and fish laid upon it and bread. "Come and breakfast," he invited them, just as he invites us to the eucharist each morning. And none of those reclining dared ask him, "Who art thou?" knowing it was the Lord. And Jesus came and took bread and gave it to them and likewise the fish. When, therefore, they had breakfasted, Jesus said to Simon Peter, "Simon, son of John, dost thou love me?" He said to him, "Yes, Lord, thou knowest that I love thee." He said to him, "Feed my sheep, take care of my flock."

REFLECTION AND DISCUSSION

1. How can you prepare for mass in order to deepen your experience of Christ's presence? Consider the attitude you will bring with you and the difference it will make in your openness.

2. Reflect on the extension of the Eucharistic celebration of the mass throughout the hours and days of your life afterwards.

CHAPTER 16

Learning Charity Through Christ

On the night of the Last Supper, our Blessed Lord reminded us, "If you love me, keep my commandments" (Jn 14:15). In any covenant of love it is presumed that each party will do all in one's power to please the beloved. In each covenant of love into which God has entered with humankind, there have been certain requirements to be fulfilled by us in order to please God. On Mt. Sinai God revealed to Moses the commandments that the Hebrews were to keep in order to be the chosen people. There followed an exchange of promises between God and the assembly of the elect which was irrevocably sealed in blood. God promised to be faithful to the chosen people, to protect them from their enemies, to bring them to the promised land and to help them gain possession of it. The assembly of the chosen ones promised to show their love for God by obeying the commandments. Because the Jews were still in an early stage of their relationship with God, the commandments of the Old Testament were limited to minimum requirements and worded in a negative way. This was the most God could expect at that time.

With the coming of Jesus, another covenant of love was made between the heavenly Father/Mother and the Christian community. New promises were exchanged between God and the new family of God's people. This exchange of vows was sealed in the blood of Christ upon the cross. Not only did the God-Man promise to bring the people to the Kingdom of God on the Last Day, he promised to lay down his life for them. "Greater love than this, no one has, that one lay down his life for his friends" (Jn 15:13). Likewise, the people of God are expected to do considerably more than the chosen people of the Old Testament. "A new commandment I give you, that you love one another as I have loved you" (Jn 13:34). As Christians, the standard by which we must measure our love for our neighbor is the unlimited love which Jesus Christ has for us.

The commitment of faith is the beginning of our response of love to God's call of grace in the New Testament. To persevere in our love we make use of Christian hope to give us the courage to keep progressing towards our goal of perfect union with God. The virtue of Christian charity is the perfection and completion of the love that we have been commanded by Christ to have and to give to others. This fullness of love is not only to be given to God, but also to our neighbor. "As long as you did it for one of these, the least of my brethren, you did it for me" (Mt 25:40). Until the coming of Jesus, it was impossible for God to ask this kind of love from us. Love is something that we can learn only through the actual experience of being loved by another person. It was necessary that Christ give us the example of the love that is expected of us, his brothers and sisters. Charity, therefore, is a virtue that only those who possess deep faith and enduring hope are able to practice it.

Let no one imagine that it is easy to practice Christian charity. Besides the special helping grace from God, there is need of great effort on our part to rise to this supernatural level of love. Charity is the incarnation of the natural virtue of love and to attain it requires free consent and cooperation of both God and ourselves. Through the sacraments we are given the necessary grace from God to attain this new standard of love: Christ's love for us. As one Christian feast succeeds another and as one liturgical year follows another, the community of God's chosen people should have many encounters of love with the God-Man, Jesus Christ. Through our participation in the actions of the Mystical Body of Christ from day to day, we will get to know from first-hand experience what it means to be loved by God in human form.

A lifetime of effort on our part is necessary in order to attain the degree of love which the New Covenant of Christ requires. This should be considered a challenge rather than a reason for discouragement. In these present "between-times," before the final coming of Christ, we are to prepare ourselves for the third aeon. The full life only begins on the Last Day when Christ will establish his permanent Kingdom. We are expected to work hard to cooperate with the graces of God that are given us and to advance each day a step nearer to the fullness of a Christ-like love. As long as we keep progressing toward perfect love, we should be happy. We need only be concerned when, year after year, we can see no real progress in the intensity of our love for God and others. Love is a living thing and so never remains the same for very long. If we are not advancing in love, we can be sure that somewhere in our life our love is decaying.

What can we do to make sure that our love for God and neighbor becomes more Christ-like? If our knowledge and love of Christ grows a little each day, then both consciously and unconsciously our love for others will more and more resemble the love of Christ. It is impossible to love another sincerely and deeply without at the same time imitating him. If we desire to fulfill our part of the New Covenant, we need to progress through all five steps of love in our relationship with Christ. Jesus must become the focal point of everything in our life. His Incarnation is the origin of all the graces that have come to us from the Father. It is through him in the liturgy that we make our return of love and service to God. Through union with Christ in the sacraments and in his Mystical Body, we attain here on earth the highest possible union with God.

The first step in loving Christ is getting to know all about him. We must study and meditate upon every detail of his life until we come to know him as a real person and a true friend. Through a daily effort on our part, it is possible rather quickly for the marvelous personality of Jesus to come to life for us. We will find ourselves greatly attracted to him, absorbed by every slightest detail of his character. We will read all we can find on the subject of Jesus, if it promises to give us some new insight into his human and divine natures. After a while, we will come to have our favorite authors who in our opinion seem to have best captured the personality of Jesus. We will love to read their books again and again, meditating long afterwards on the picture they give us of Jesus. However, we will turn more and more to the four Gospel books of the New Testament. By now we will know enough about the character of Jesus to read and interpret for ourselves the deeper meaning of Jesus' words and actions. We will enjoy comparing the texts of Matthew, Mark, Luke and John in a harmony of the Gospels, picking out every detail given by each of the evangelists. The Gospels will become love-letters to us from our beloved Jesus. We will want to read them again and again, each time with greater comprehension than in previous readings. Once caught by the magnetic personality of Jesus, we will never want to forsake him.

While growing in the understanding and appreciation of Christ, we will begin to make comparisons between his character and our own. The greater the contrast between the way Christ spoke and acted and our behavior, the more we will realize the need of change on our part. This is the second step of love where we desire to open ourselves to the beloved so that he may know us as we really are. We don't want to hide anything from him or from ourselves. Seeing the honesty and straightforwardness of Jesus, we will want to imitate his frankness and sincerity. Through learning to know Jesus, we will learn to know ourselves and to recognize what we need to do in order to be like him.

The third step of love called benevolence will also have been growing apace with our increased love of Jesus. Our hearts go out instinctively towards an object that the intellect presents as being good. Therefore, every step in our knowledge of the infinite goodness of Christ will result in an increased desire to please and imitate him. Our love for Christ will cause us to study how he served others, so that we can do likewise. In this fourth stage of love, we unite with Jesus as our Christ; we are unified. We will take seriously his command to love others as he loves us and our lives will begin gradually to grow in unselfish service for others.

The desire for union with Jesus will make us long for that ultimate union with him in the Kingdom of God.

We will not be content to wait so long but will seek every opportunity to become one with him here and now, looking forward with eager longing to every participation in the liturgy, especially the Eucharist. Having studied the Word of God in the Gospels, we will want to partake of this Word made flesh in the Eucharist. Our Eucharistic union will in turn make us want to extend this union with Christ through charity for our sisters and brothers, the members of the Mystical Body of Christ. In these expressions of the fifth level of love, we live the transcendental qualities of God. Our lives are evidence of the value of truth, justice, goodness, unity and beauty.

Another way of continuing the union with Christ is through loving conversation with him, either in the presence of the Blessed Sacrament or anywhere during the day. Knowing that we carry him within us by grace, we will find great joy and satisfaction in speaking to him whenever we are alone. When in the presence of others, our faith will tell us that Jesus is also present among us. As Jesus says, "Where two or three gather in my name, there I am in the midst" (Mt 18:20). We are able to show reverence and love for our brother Christ by the respect and service we give to his brothers and sisters. Jesus is one friend we never need fear of losing. "Behold I am with you all days, even unto the consummation of the world" (Mt 28:20). "I will not leave you orphans; I will come to you ... In that day you will know that I am in the Father, you in me and I in you ... He who loves me will be loved by my Father and I will love him and manifest myself to him" (Jn 14:18-21).

REFLECTION AND DISCUSSION

1. In whose life do you see the transcendental qualities of love expressing their unity with Christ? What can you learn from the wisdom of their life?

2. Has your journey of love stalled somewhere? Considering the endless love of God, what will you do about it?

CHAPTER 17

The Beatitudes: New Commandments of Christ

In the Old Testament, God was content with a minimum of compliance to the Ten Commandments, but with the coming of Christ much more is expected. "You are to be perfect, even as your heavenly Father is perfect" (Mt 6:48). We are to model our life and service upon the life and actions of Jesus Christ. We are to submit our whole being to God as did Jesus. In the Sermon on the Mount we are given the new commandments required for the new Covenant. God, through Moses, asked the people of God to promise obedience to the commandments of Mt. Sinai. Jesus Christ, on another mountain in Galilee, asked his disciples to live according to the new law of perfection found in the Gospels. The obligations of Christian charity are often called counsels instead of commandments to emphasize the fact that God wants them to be motivated by love rather than fear. These counsels are addressed to all Christian followers of Jesus and not merely to some elite group of Christians. There is no place for fence sitters or those who choose to be mediocre in the Kingdom of Christ. When our love is sincere, half-measures are impossible in our commitment to Christ. "You shall love the Lord your God with your *whole heart*, with your *whole soul*, with your *whole strength* and with your *whole mind*" (Lk 10:27).

To appreciate how exceedingly higher are the requirements of love for Christians than for those of the Old

Testament, it is useful to compare the Mosaic commandments with the Gospel counsels in the Sermon on the Mount. God commanded the Israelites not to worship false gods; we are commanded to love God with the same love as did Jesus. Moses forbade cursing; we are urged to simplify our speech to "yes and no". The primary obligation of the Jewish Sabbath was to refrain from work. We are urged to use our Sunday leisure to perform the work of divine love called the Eucharist and to carry out other works of charity towards our neighbor. The Old Law forbade murder; Jesus asks us not even to be angry with our neighbor. Moses forbade stealing; Jesus urges us, "go, sell whatever you have and give to the poor" (Mk 10:21). The Jews were forbidden to lie; the New Law expects the same openness and honesty as we see in Jesus. "Learn of me for I am meek and humble of heart" (Mt 11:29). The Israelites were told not to covet their neighbor's wife or goods. We are told to be willing to give away everything in our love for others.

As Christians, our model in loving and serving is Jesus. To carry out his heroic charity we need abundant grace from God. Christ, having commanded these things, will most certainly give us the means to perform them. However, the accomplishment of Christian charity will not follow automatically from the bestowal of divine grace. We must cooperate in order to reach the heroic level of charity expected of us. This high level is made clear to us in the eight beatitudes which form the Magna Charta of the Sermon on the Mount and the whole Christian religion.

Blessed are the Poor in Spirit,
Theirs is the Kingdom of God

The poor in spirit are those who are keenly aware of their lack of goodness. This implies a high degree of self-knowledge, which comes only to those who are able to face up to themselves as they really are in God's sight. This poverty of spirit gives us a wonderful freedom from pride and vanity and is the necessary preparation for union with God. Having emptied our souls of excessive preoccupation with ourselves, we are now open to the graces of God. Being aware of our own lack of goodness, we become beggars of the Holy Spirit for the needed help from God. Only those humble enough to realize their own poverty are able to find room in their hearts for Christ. Having opened their hearts to Christ's love, they are assured in this beatitude that God will give them the Kingdom of grace. This Kingdom will begin already in this second aeon, for "...theirs is the Kingdom of God."

Blessed are the Meek
for They Shall Possess the Earth

Meekness here means sensitivity to everything of God's—God's will, love, Spirit. Just as the strings of a sensitive violin vibrate the same notes that are struck upon a nearby piano, so the meek person responds instantly to every indication of God's will. This is the meekness of Jesus: "I do always the things that are pleasing to my Father" (Jn 8:29).

To attain this meekness our minds and hearts must be completely open to truth, both natural and supernatural.

We must be able to distinguish the inner voice of God's Spirit from the destructive voice of our pride. We need to free ourselves from the blindness and distractions created by selfish attachments to creatures. Through loving Jesus and others we will make our hearts tender and susceptible to the least movement of God's love. To attain this sensitivity we must overcome our inhibitions and repressions and cultivate a delicate response to every manifestation of truth and love. Instead of being enslaved to the things of earth, the meek have only one master, Jesus Christ, the God-Man. Independent of the world, they are the only persons capable of being true masters and possessors of the earth.

Blessed are They who Mourn for They Shall Be Comforted

When Jesus drew near to Jerusalem on his last journey, he wept over the city. "If you had known the things that are for your peace. But now they are hidden from your eyes" (Lk 19:42). Anyone who is filled with the love of Good will sincerely mourn at the sight of the evil, the violence and the suffering that is present in today's world. Our anguish of spirit must be an honest suffering that comes from love and not merely from anger or hatred. Suffering motivated by love deepens and broadens our whole personality and the cross then becomes a stepping-stone to a higher level of existence. By means of God's helping graces our mourning becomes an experience of incarnation that lifts us up into a greater union of love with God. In the possession of this greater charity we find a deep peace and comfort. Our faith enables us to see the value of suffering. Our Christian hope gives us here and now a joyful anticipation of the goal of the future Kingdom.

Blessed are They Who Hunger and Thirst for Justice for They Shall Be Satisfied

Another word for justice is holiness or righteousness. Justice means to give to everyone what is their due. That includes God, neighbor and self. Therefore, a just person will be a holy and righteous person. If we love Jesus, we will have something of his intense desire for justice. Our desire to see that everyone is given what is due to them will be similar to the craving of a starving man in search of food. We will want to see God's will fulfilled on earth with the same intensity as a man dying of thirst longs for water. We will experience no peace in ourselves unless we are constantly striving with every fiber of our being to see that justice is done to everyone. This means a desire to see that God is given the honor, love and service that is due to Him/Her. In our desire for the coming of God's Kingdom we will go to any extreme to do our part to accomplish it, both in ourselves and in others. As long as there is any injustice anywhere in the world, we will not be satisfied until it has been righted. Our Lord tells us that it is a great blessing to possess this intense craving for justice. S/He promises that if we persevere in our desires and implement them as best we can by our actions, then we will live to see justice accomplished. God never gives a desire without making available the means to fulfill it. If we are willing to pay the price for justice, we shall surely be satisfied. The price Jesus paid for justice was his death on the cross. If we wish to be his follower, we need to be willing to lay down our life in order to quench our thirst for justice.

Blessed are the Merciful for They Shall Obtain Mercy

Our mercy to our neighbor is similar to meekness toward God. The meek possess the earth while the merciful give it away to their neighbor. If we give mercy to others, we will surely receive mercy from God, since love is never lost by being shared. Instead spiritual goods become multiplied when we share them with others. Meekness makes us sensitive to the will of God; mercy renders us sensitive to the needs of our neighbor. To do this we have to overcome our egotism that blinds us to the needs of everyone except ourselves. With understanding and sympathy we learn to feel the calamities endured by others as though they were our own. Through the love of Christ we identify ourselves as completely as possible with others. Through grace we reach the point of saying with Christ, "what you do to one of these, the least of my brothers and sisters, you do unto me." To have attained this identity of love with our neighbor is proof of a similar identity of love with Christ. Through mercy we share all that we have with others. At the same time we merit a share in all the possessions of Christ. To give mercy is to receive mercy.

Blessed are the Pure of Heart
for They Shall See God

The purity of heart in the Sermon on the Mount means considerably more than sexual chastity. Negatively, it is the absence of selfishness and pride. Positively, it is the power to see God and good everywhere we look. "For the pure, all things are pure" (Tit 1:15). Instead of seeing evil, the pure of heart see the possibilities of good in everyone and every event. A pure heart is a creative heart, capable of bringing good out of the least thing, even out of evil. "For those who love God, all things will work together unto good" (Rom 8:28). Purity of heart is not an easy process during this second aeon. We must work hard to purify our own lives of all evil. Only then will we be able to see with a clear eye the potential for good in others. To see God in a sinner will mean to see the wonderful capacity for good in that person. To bring forth this good, will require great pains of labor on our part as well as the other person. However, if we have succeeded through patient suffering to transform the evil in ourselves into good, then we will have gained a proficiency to help others do likewise. To attain purity of heart we will need many graces from God and the first grace for which to ask is the light to see the possibilities for good in each of our faults. With this knowledge, we will be able to face up to the full truth about ourselves without anger, denial or discouragement— only the determination to turn the mistakes of the past into a future good. The energy behind hatred and evil is the same energy that is needed for love. We need only to change the direction of this energy from an evil goal and unto a new direction of love and goodness.

Blessed are the Peacemakers,
They Shall Be Called Children of God

Peace is the tranquility of order: when everything and everyone is in its proper place, we have peace. It is our task as disciples of Jesus to help establish peace between God and sinners; between others and ourselves; between neighbor and neighbor; between the various aspects of our own personality; between body and soul; between nature and grace; between individual and community. This work of peacemaking is a priestly work since a priest is primarily a reconciler of persons who have become alienated from each other. There is no greater power given to human beings than the power to bring peace, love and joy between God and human beings or between alienated persons on earth. Those who share with Jesus in this task of peacemaking will be the ones who directly work to prepare this earth for the third aeon. Peace will never be attained by compromise or cowardice. It will be found only through the incarnation of everything natural into the supernatural level of grace. In this sense a peacemaker is a co-creator with God in building the Kingdom of renewed creation. For those who are successful in this difficult task of peacemaking, there is a great danger of pride. Therefore we must stay humble and accept our place as children of God and be ever mindful that all good comes from God.

Blessed are They Who Suffer Persecution
for Sake of Justice for Theirs is the Kingdom of God

Not every persecution is a blessing but only that which results from our efforts to please God and to work for justice. If we are successful in pleasing God, we will arouse the fury of God's enemies. Those who are satisfied with their mediocrity will resist us because we disturb them with the intensity of our love. The slothful who resist all change will persecute us because we upset their comfort and security. Egocentric persons will see us as an enemy and do all in their power to destroy us. We will be considered as dangerous innovators, a threat to the status quo and to their own peace. However, we need not fear this kind of opposition. Instead of harming us, it purifies us of our selfishness and speeds up our growth in wholeness and maturity. They will seek to kill us, only to find that we rise each time from the tomb more glorious than ever. Just as Jesus redeemed the world through suffering and death, so we will continue the work of the world's redemption through our suffering and death at the hands of our persecutors. "For those who love God, all things work together unto good ... for those whom God has foreknown, He has also predestined to become conformed to the image of His Son" (Rom 8:28-29).

REFLECTION AND DISCUSSION

1. In which beatitude have you struggled for years? Identify one step to take, pray, and begin your effort toward wholeness with renewed resolve and the assurance of God's grace.

2. Which beatitude represents an area in which you have grown? Pray for an opportunity to share that wisdom with a fellow pilgrim.

CHAPTER 18

The Gifts of the Holy Spirit

In our progress towards union with God, we need not
only natural virtues. We have an even greater need of
the supernatural virtues of faith, hope and charity.
Growth in these latter virtues is primarily the work of
the Holy Spirit. The gifts of the Holy Spirit are at work
in every soul that is in the state of grace, but less no-
ticeably in the early stages of our journey of faith. As
one progresses toward sanctity, the seven gifts of the
Spirit become more and more evident. They are especially observable in the community of God's people
whenever there is a crisis that requires the special intervention of God. If the people cooperate with the Holy
Spirit at these times, there will be a tremendous advance
of the whole community toward the completion of
God's Kingdom. Each gift of the Spirit is a grace that
we are free to accept or refuse. Lest these gifts be lost
through ignorance, it is essential that we know all we
can about the workings of the Spirit so that we can recognize them when offered and do our best to cooperate
with them.

Fear of the Lord

This gift is needed very specially at the beginning of our
journey of faith. Through it we realize the vast distance
that separates God from us and thus we appreciate what

a terrible thing it is to flaunt oneself against the creator through disobedience to the divine will. This gift gives us an understanding of the infinite transcendence of God above the whole of creation. When it is working in our souls, we show the proper reverence for God in prayer and worship. By means of our normal, natural knowledge of God we can understand something of divine omnipotence. The Holy Spirit takes this natural awesomeness and transforms it into a beautiful personal relationship of reverent love for all the things of God. If we cooperate with the gift of Fear of the Lord, our humility grows each day. Without discouragement we are able to accept the truth of our nothingness apart from God and our absolute dependence upon God and all it means to be God's creatures. With this reverence for God in our hearts, temptations to pride and egocentricity are more easily conquered and the attractions of forbidden pleasures no longer allure us. All of our relationships with God, especially prayer and worship, will be filled with the deep reverence which a creature owes to the Lord and Creator of all. Each time we pray the Lord's Prayer we pray for this gift of fear of the Lord when we pray, "Hallowed be thy name."

Piety

The gift of piety balances fear of the Lord by revealing to us that God is our heavenly parent (a divine Mother-Father) as well as our Lord and Creator. By means of this gift we appreciate all it means to be a child of God. Even though we are vividly aware of the infinite greatness of our heavenly parent and our own nothingness, through the power of this gift we approach God on the most intimate terms of love. We realize that the primary relationship which God desires with us is not fear but the love of a parent and child. In our natural relationship with God, there must be a balance between the awesome and the fascinating sides of God's nature. The twin gifts of fear of the Lord and piety give us this balance in our love and thus perfect our nature. Love for all our friends should increase as we realize that we are all children of the same heavenly Parent. Our prayer life improves as Piety encourages us to speak most intimately and lovingly to each of the Persons of the Holy Trinity. This gift is needed especially during the long desert journey of what St. John of the Cross calls the Dark Night. Convinced by the Holy Spirit of God's fatherly and motherly love, care and protection for us, we find the courage to progress more quickly across the dry deserts of our spiritual life towards the bright hope of the promised land of perfect love.

Counsel

This is the gift that perfects the natural virtue of prudence. It is a divine intuition that enables us to know God's will in all our words and actions. Through this gift, the Holy Spirit exerts a sweet compulsion upon our minds, giving us God's conscience of what is right and wrong in a given situation. It tells us when to speak or act and when to be quiet and do nothing. Without any process of human reasoning, we are given a divine practical judgment for the particular matter at hand. Previously we may have been completely in the dark, but at the given moment for acting, we are shown the right word to say and the right action to take. Counsel becomes especially necessary when we are choosing the particular vocation and work to which God is calling us.

At times the gift of Counsel clouds our minds so that we are left hesitant, confused and unable to act. If we are patient, accept the humiliation and remain full of confidence in God, some event of divine providence will occur to set us right. Through this gift we will be shown the right time for everything. By means of counsel, the Holy Spirit will show us how to be both firm and gentle, merciful and just, considerate and strict, truthful yet prudent. We will be given the wisdom to know how to keep secrets and still speak without telling a lie.

Fortitude

It is not enough to know what to say or do, we need the courage to act upon the light which the Holy Spirit gives us. The gift of Fortitude is the supernatural incarnation of the natural virtue of fortitude and courage. It is also the perfection of the virtue of Christian hope. Natural courage alone is not enough to enable us to cooperate with supernatural Counsel and Knowledge. The gift of Fortitude is needed in times of crisis when courageous decisions must be made. Often it is only by the help of the Holy Spirit that we find the strength to leave our old, accustomed ways and rise to a higher level of maturity and sanctity. Fortitude is needed most of all when a soul is suffering the dark nights of struggle that must be endured in order to reach the heights of heroic charity. Without the special help of the Holy Spirit no soul can arrive in the higher mansions of passive contemplation and the unitive way. By this gift of Fortitude we are given the courage of God Him/Herself to overcome the

difficulties that naturally would be impossible to conquer. Counsel and Knowledge bring reason to perfection, while Fortitude perfects the will and the passions.
In this gift we receive the grace to suffer with Christ
whatever agony it is God's will to permit us. At times
we are left weak and prostrate like Jesus in Gethsemane;
but at the right moment heavenly strength is given us so
that we can, like the martyrs, endure the greatest possible suffering with joy and peace, provided we cooperate.

Knowledge

This gift enables us to see the things of this world as
God sees them. This "new look" makes clear many former mysteries in our life. One no longer needs to keep
asking, "Why did God do this?" "Why did this have to
happen to me?" By some kind of divine intuition, we
begin to see the reason for most of the things that happen. There will still be mysteries in God's dealings with
humankind, but as one progresses in grace, these mysteries become less and less. At the moment of the event,
one may not be able to see the loving hand of God's
providence. However, if acts of faith and hope are
made, in due time the Holy Spirit will reveal some good
reasons why it was for the best. Through this gift of
Knowledge, we more and more understand the truth of
St. Paul's words, "For those who love God, all things
work together unto good" (Rom 8:28).

Thanks to this gift, all of life becomes filled with joy
and enthusiasm. One awakens each morning with delight that another day of God's grace has been given us.
One arises with new energy from the Holy Spirit to

tackle whatever problems the new day brings, knowing that the same God who has shown such wonderful care in the past, will be there to help us today. Through the gift of Knowledge we are able to experience first-hand the providence of God. Seeing the things of earth in the light of divine truth, we lose our fears of God, of people, of the future, of ourselves. This gift perfects the virtue of faith by giving us a supernatural "Extra Sensory Perception." Blindly but in reality nevertheless, we develop a certain intuition for the presence of God in each thing and each event of our life. Through Knowledge the Holy Spirit shows us the value of our humiliations, failures, temptations, persecutions and sufferings of all kinds. Things which nature presents to us as evil, may now appear as good.

The gift of Knowledge enables us to put a proper order into our lives and the lives of those under us. It shows us the true value of each thing and its relationship to God and our goal of the Kingdom of God. At one time Knowledge gives us a distaste for creatures, when their attraction is a threat to our life of wholeness. At another time it will show us the wonderful beauties of God in nature and in creatures. All of our poetical and artistic abilities are enhanced through this gift, since it enables us to see the divine hand in everything of nature. Our practical judgments of the things of earth benefit greatly through this gift of the Spirit. Progress in maturity and wholeness is especially aided by this gift.

Understanding

The gift of Knowledge gives us God's insight concerning the things of creation, while Understanding enlightens us in the mysteries of our faith. Souls in higher mansions of the Unitive Way are especially gifted with this grace of Understanding. Through this gift we are given new insights into Sacred Scripture and the teachings of the Church, seeing things that in the past we never suspected. Understanding enables us to penetrate the veils of faith and opens to us many new dimensions of revealed truth in the Bible. Without any dependence upon earthly images, the Spirit fills the mind with an intuitive knowledge of the divine life shared by Father, Son and Holy Spirit. This blinding, supernatural light of the Holy Spirit may leave the soul still wrapped in mystery, unable to find words to express what was revealed. Through the gift of Understanding one is given unshakable convictions about the reality of God and the mysteries of our faith. Although still living in the darkness of the second aeon, a soul filled with Understanding will possess great joy and peace in the possession of God's truth. "Oh the depth of the riches, of the wisdom and of the knowledge of God" (Rom 11:33).

Those persons engaged in religious education as well as those who are studying theology, sacred scripture and religion need to pray for this gift of Understanding. The homilist in each Sunday's liturgy needs to be open to this gift and pray fervently for Understanding before attempting to break open the message of the Word of God for God's people. This is the special gift of the Holy Spirit which will unlock and open for us the doors of all the mysteries of God given us by divine revelation.

Wisdom

The greatest of all the gifts of the Holy Spirit is Wisdom, the perfection of the virtue of charity. It enables a soul to find joy only in loving God and is a foretaste of the joys of heaven and the third aeon. Wisdom gives a soul a supernatural relish and delight for God and all the things of God. "Taste and see how good the Lord is" (Ps 34:9). Having tasted the joys of the Lord, one can no longer find satisfaction in the things of the earth apart from God. One now feels completely at home with the Lord and the only happiness is to possess God's love more and more. Wisdom enables a soul to embrace with sincere delight everything of God's will and to find peace and joy in the very midst of pain, suffering, humiliation, persecution and death. By this gift the final purifying of the soul is completed and one is ready to enter immediately into God's presence at the moment of death. Although present somewhat in all the levels of faith, it is possessed most fully in the spiritual marriage of the seventh and highest mansion of grace. Through the outpouring of Wisdom the whole community of God's people is now able to progress more swiftly toward their final fulfillment in the Kingdom of the Last Day.

REFLECTION AND DISCUSSION

1. Which of the gifts of the Holy Spirit appeal to you the most? How can you nurture your gift(s) and use them for the greater glory of God

2. Name a person in your parish, or in the culture at large, who models gifts of the Spirit. Thank God for their witness and reflect on what you see in them which you can rightly imitate to grow in wholeness.

CHAPTER 19

The Fruits of the Holy Spirit

Our Lord tells us in the Sermon on the Mount, "By their fruits you shall know them" (Mt 7:16). The working of the gifts of the Holy Spirit is often unconscious and unknown even to ourselves. This is especially true of the higher gifts of Wisdom, Understanding, Counsel and Fortitude. Usually they work in such beautiful cooperation with our natural powers that it is often impossible to distinguish between nature and grace. However, if we put no serious obstacles to the activity of the gifts of the Spirit it will not be long before the fruits of the Spirit will become evident in our lives and to those with whom we live. The more we progress in the life of grace, the more manifest will be these fruits. We have twelve such fruits, following St. Jerome's version of Galatians 5:22-23. They are: charity, joy, peace, patience, kindness, generosity, gentleness, faithfulness, moderation, self-control, purity, chastity.

Everyone living in grace should enjoy something of each of these blessings of the Holy Spirit. In the earlier stages of our faith journey we may expect only an occasional experience of the fruits. As we progress toward wholeness and sanctity the results of the work of the Spirit within our life become more open and constant. In a really whole and holy person the enjoyment of the fruits should be so great and continuous that the words of St. Catherine of Siena are quite applicable: "All the way to heaven is heaven too." In this sense, through the experience of these fruits of the Holy Spirit we can already here on earth begin to experience some of the blessings of heaven. The life in heaven after death will be an ever deepening and everlasting possession of the fruits of the Spirit. Any valid growth in one or the other of these fruits is definite proof that we are on the right road toward our goal of sanctity. We have here twelve tests by which we can determine whether we are being led by the good Spirit and not by some other spirit opposed to God.

Charity or Agapic Love

The first of these tests is called charity and it will ever be the most distinguishing mark of a true follower of Jesus Christ. Charity is a very special Christian virtue which goes exceedingly deep, beyond any purely natural love. To distinguish this Christian love from natural, human love it has been given either the name "charity" (from the Latin word, "caritas" meaning dearness or high value) or "agapic love" (from the Greek word "agape" meaning love or a love feast). To possess this agapic love means to love both God and neighbor in the same way that Jesus Christ loved God and others. The whole New Testament is filled with examples of this greatest of the fruits of the Spirit. If we are growing in grace, it should be apparent both to ourselves and to others that our charity is constantly increasing. We may be able to see this growth only from year to year. But as we progress into the higher levels of faith the rate of increase in agapic love should become faster and faster. Anyone who does not experience a more or less constant expansion of one's charity toward God and neighbor should be concerned about one's state of spiritual health.

Through the gifts of Understanding and Counsel the Holy Spirit reveals to us what our divine spouse desires of us in the area of charity. Because God is such a tremendous lover, the divine demands of love are exceedingly great. In all truth we must learn to love God to the same reckless degree that Jesus loved his heavenly "Abba" (Daddy). We must learn to love others to the same heroic degree that Jesus loved his disciples, ready and willing to give his life for them. To experience this first of the fruits of the Spirit we need to study, meditate and pray every day on the words of Jesus in the four Gospels and on each of the events of the life of Jesus as they are recorded in the Gospels. The other books of the New Testament—Acts of Apostles, Epistles of Paul, Peter, James and John—have much to teach us about Christian charity or agapic love. A thorough knowledge of these books of the New Testament will give us many tests to determine if we are truly experiencing this first of the fruits of the Holy Spirit.

Joy

Our whole life of grace is meant to be a joyful experience. Due to our weakness and failures, the way to perfect joy has many ups and downs. Nevertheless, as one progresses toward holiness one will become more and more aware of a constantly increasing joy of the spirit. As we grow in grace we should gradually find more and more joy in thinking about God and the things of God. One of the areas where this joy will especially be experienced is in our prayer-life. Even though one will frequently be tested by dryness and distractions, if one perseveres, the joys of the Spirit will be manifest by a very optimistic, positive attitude towards everything and everyone. Through an ever fuller experience of the virtue of hope, one experiences a joyful contentment even in midst of pain.

Pleasure is a very superficial and passing phenomenon that is entirely different from this fruit of joy. Pleasure and suffering are totally contradictory, but this is not true of suffering and joy. As we progress towards holiness not only do these alternate with one another in taking possession of the spirit of a person, but they are frequently present at one and the same time. This is one of those Christian paradoxes that we see present so often in the lives of the saints. In the midst of the greatest possible persecution and suffering, the martyrs, for example, experienced the most intense joy. The Canticle of the three Hebrews in the fiery furnace celebrates one such experience of joy in suffering (Dan 3:24-90). Because all this is so contrary to the normal experience of nature, the fruit of joy in times of distress and pain is one of the best of all signs of the presence of the Holy Spirit within our souls. Anyone can be happy when all is going well; it is only those living in God's grace who are able to possess their souls in sincere joy even in the midst of pain. Those who have been given this fruit of joy should be ever grateful to God.

Peace

This fruit is closely akin to that of joy. St. Augustine, in his work *City of God,* defines peace as the tranquility of order. Therefore peace is the fruit of justice. When everything is in its right place and proper order and everyone has been given all that is due to them, there should be peace. Jesus at his resurrection on Easter Sunday clearly indicates that peace is one of the fruits of the Holy Spirit. Jesus came on earth to reestablish peace and order between God and humanity. Every sin is a disorder of the relationship of love that should exist between ourselves and God or between ourselves and other human beings. It is the work of the Holy Spirit to give us the tranquility of a beautiful and orderly relationship of love with God and our neighbor. This will be accomplished through forgiveness and mercy. If we abandon ourselves completely to the Holy Spirit, we will gradually experience an ever greater peace. This fruit of the Spirit is purchased at the price of sacrificing our will to the will of God. The real disorder in the world that destroys peace is the rebellion against God in the human will. We may imagine that we will find peace and satisfaction in doing our own will. Actually, the very opposite is true.

The joy of a good conscience leaves our soul very much at peace. We are able to face the problems of life peacefully as long as we know that everything is in its proper order. Even in the midst of the greatest pain and suffering, it is possible to find oneself at peace with God, with others and with ourselves, provided we are convinced that we are doing God's will. The example of our peace of soul becomes a great inspiration to those around us. If it is a true peace of the Spirit, it will persist regardless of the external circumstances of our life.

Patience

A fruit of the Spirit closely allied to peace is patience. How delightful it is to ourselves and to all those with whom we live if we have been given this wonderful grace of patience—patience with ourselves, with others and with God. There can be a natural patience that is due either to one's disposition or to the strenuous efforts made to conquer our temper. However, this particular fruit will be experienced at times and places where there is no natural explanation for its existence. It is quite evident that it is something entirely beyond one's own efforts. It is simply the power of the Holy Spirit which enables us to rise above the natural situation and meet it with the patience of God. Those who possess this fruit will know how to wait patiently upon the movements of God's grace. Despite their intense desire to grow in love and sanctity, they will be patient with the Lord when God sees fit to delay His/Her coming. This same patience will be shown with oneself, one's faults and failures. One will strive manfully to grow daily in love, yet be willing to keep working despite the many years of slow progress. Finally, their relation with others will more and more be governed by an unlimited patience with their faults and mistakes. Despite every appearance to the contrary, they will continue to hope for the best and to help everyone who comes to them. This fruit of patience is one that can be more easily observed than almost any one of the other fruits. For this reason it is especially valuable as a test to determine whether we are progressing in the life of grace.

Kindness

This is another fruit that can be easily observed both in ourselves and others. If we are growing in grace, our sincere kindness and compassion toward others will be more and more apparent. Without any natural reason, we will find ourselves able to be kind to those whom naturally we might be expected to dislike. It is evident that this is the work of the Spirit in the depths of our soul. How fortunate we are when we have the privilege to live with a person who has attained this fruit of the Spirit. We can be sure of their great kindness and compassion toward us, regardless of what we do or how we might fail them. We feel a great security and trust when we are in their presence. Also, we can be sure that our reputation is secure in our absence, provided such a person is present. Through their example, we ourselves find the courage to return to the struggle needed to attain to heights of love to which we have been called by God's providence.

Generosity

As a person grows in wholeness and holiness, one becomes more and more generous in sharing one's time, talents, energy, experience, wisdom, money and possessions with others. One becomes keenly aware that we are only stewards of those things which belong to us and which worldly people call "their possessions." All we have is a gift of God and belongs to God. They are loaned to us to be used according to God's good pleasure. They are to be shared with others, with anyone who has need of them. Our only concern should be, how can we do the most good with all that has been entrusted by

God to us. One of the clearest signs of growth in holiness is that of an ever greater generosity and willingness to share all we have with others. With each passing year we should see ourselves becoming more and more generous and even reckless in our willingness to share everything we have with others. Following the example of St. Francis of Assisi and many other saints, the hope would be that when we come to die we will have given away everything we possess or over which we have control.

Gentleness

As a person grows in grace, a wonderful balance results in all the diverse sides of one's character. It is usually difficult to determine the natural temperament of those who are holy because the Holy Spirit has compensated for those things lacking in nature. An example of this is the fruit of gentleness that begins to appear in the life of a holy person who earlier in life may have been quite severe. Through the power of the Holy Spirit, all the best qualities of both masculinity and femininity will be present in those who have progressed in wholeness and holiness. It is especially beautiful when someone who is eminently masculine is found to be filled with a deep tenderness and gentleness towards all those in need. It is so far beyond the natural expectations that we have good evidence of the presence of the Spirit. A gentle person realizes that not everything is either black or white, but there are many gray areas in life. Therefore, one should refrain from making absolute judgments or statements but show great tolerance towards those who see things differently from oneself. Isaiah expresses this fruit of gentleness in the first of the Servant songs: "The bruised reed he will not break, the smoking wick he will not extinguish" (Is 42:3).

Faithfulness

When we look for a friend, we want someone whom we can trust, one who is completely faithful. For this reason we should try to choose our friends among those who have perfected their natural dispositions of trust-worthiness as well as enjoying the fruit of a supernatural fidelity. As one grows in grace-life, people will come more and more to depend upon such a person, knowing that s/he is always dependable and can be trusted. They can always be counted upon to do the right thing when handling a difficult situation. This faithfulness will be seen not only in their devotion to the welfare of others, it will also be present in their fidelity to their duties to God and the duties of their state of life. If one compares one's present life with the situation as it existed previously, there should be evidence of an increase in fidelity for which there is no known natural explanation. The presumption is that it is the work of the Holy Spirit producing this fruit of faithfulness.

Moderation or Balance

Ordinarily, virtue stands in the middle between two opposite extremes. From a natural point of view the virtue of prudence is given to help us strike the right balance in each situation of life. Nevertheless, there will be many times when natural prudence is not sufficient to cope with the difficulties that arise. In these cases, the gift of

Counsel is given a soul living in grace to enable one to make the right decision. The fruit of moderation or balance will be the happy result of this gift of Counsel. It is more difficult to use something in moderation than it is to sacrifice it completely. By this fruit of moderation we will be able to strike the right balance between opposite poles of reality. Since the law of polarity is present in every area of life, this particular fruit of moderation and balance is constantly needed to keep us from becoming fanatical and going to one extreme while denying the opposite pole of reality.

Self-Control

The fruit of self-control is very similar to that of moderation and balance. In the early stages of our faith journey it requires great effort to bring one's nature under control. In the higher mansions this self-control becomes such a part of a person that it seems to be completely natural. However, one needs only to think back to the struggle that was required to attain this control of self in earlier life, and it will be clear that the Holy Spirit has been at work in our lives. Through the grace of God the energies of all our passions can be sublimated and thus incarnated into a pure, selfless love of God and neighbor.

Purity and Chastity

These final two fruits can be discussed together since chastity is simply a specific example of purity in the area of sexuality. For most people purity is considered a negative virtue because they equate it with staying away from certain forbidden things or behaviors. Our purity is measured by the degree of attraction that draws us toward the presence of God in the depths of our being. As Teilhard de Chardin says in *The Divine Milieu*, "If we love God, we love what God created, the divine milieu and all that is in it, the cosmos created by God." By this fruit of purity one attains a singleness of vision so that one can see the will of God and the hand of God in every event of one's life, in every person one encounters, in every possible situation which one might face. Jesus tells us, "if your eye be single, then your whole body will be filled with light" (Mt 6:22). The result of this fruit of purity is that our whole life becomes filled with the light of God's knowledge, God's love, God's power, God's presence. We are now able to see and judge everything from the viewpoint of God.

REFLECTION AND DISCUSSION

1. In what fruit of the spirit have you attained some understanding and practice? How can you help others to see the way to attain similar growth in this spiritual fruit?

2. If you had to name one fruit of the spirit that enabled the growth and development of other fruits, which would you name, and why? How do you see any two or three other fruits interacting synergistically in your life?

CHAPTER 20

How to Discern God's Will

One of the greatest benefits from the gifts and the fruits of the Holy Spirit is being able to practice discernment. By our openness to the gifts of the Holy Spirit we are able to discern God's will in our regard. This discernment is an exercise especially of the gift of wisdom by which the Holy Spirit enables us to see things from God's point of view. By the gift of counsel the Holy Spirit inspires us to know God's will on any given occasion. The gift of prophecy is a particular use of the gift of counsel whereby one is able to discern God's will for other persons. Understanding enables us to penetrate the mysteries of God, while knowledge helps us to penetrate the mysteries of God's providence at work in the events of history. Piety and fear of the Lord enable us to keep a good balance in our life between humility and trust. Finally, fortitude gives us the courage to carry out the will of God as revealed to us through the other six gifts.

Discernment is a process of deciding and choosing the appropriate course of action to pursue in our relationship with God, with others and toward ourselves. If we are willing to be open and receptive to the Holy Spirit, God will reveal His will through our conscience, our common sense, our past experience, the counsel of others, the Holy Scriptures as well as through special graces and insights.

Discernment should be one of the main goals of our daily period of formal prayer. Through prayer we seek to make contact with God in order to discern His will for us. If we are willing to spend some prime time each day in prayer and sincerely seek to know God's will, we may confidently expect God to reveal His will to us in one way or another. A good habit to develop is to take ten minutes each morning shortly after awakening in order to reflect upon the people we will be meeting that day and the activities planned for the day. We ask God for enlightenment to know His will and pray that we will carry out His will with every person we meet and every activity of the day. Relying on the help of the Holy Spirit, we try to discern exactly what might be God's will for us that day.

Our life and destiny might be compared to a ball of twine which is portioned out to us a little bit at a time. The providence of God reveals only a few inches of our life's destiny each day. It is impossible for us to see very far ahead what is contained in our ball of twine. We have to be alert and open constantly to the Holy Spirit in order to ascertain God's will for us each day. We do this by daily prayer, reflection, silence, consultation with others, common sense and past experience.

Each of us has a different ball of twine to unravel. We must be careful not to follow the ball of twine of someone else. When we attempt to follow the destiny of someone other than ourselves, we mess up God's whole plan in our regard. We can learn much from studying and observing the destiny of others, but we need to respect the unique destiny to which each of us has been called. The life of Christ and the lives of the saints can teach us many wonderful lessons, but God expects something different from each of us. We need the help of God's grace to discern our unique destiny and then the courage or fortitude to follow that destiny to the end of our life.

One of the first tasks in discerning our personal destiny is to see where we are over-identifying with the particular role we are now playing in society and thus losing sight of our total identity. All of us have certain specific tasks and roles to perform each day. However, our overall destiny in life is much larger than the specific role we are now playing. We need constantly to discern in prayer this greater purpose to which God is calling us.

Each of us has a significance in the overall plan of God for the human race. Everyone is important and needed. Life might be compared to a giant symphony orchestra in which each of us has our own special instrument to play and our own special musical score. If we try to use someone else's score, rather than our own, we create cacophony instead of symphony. Our true destiny will always be a balanced tension between opposite poles of reality. When we deny one pole of truth or put too much emphasis on just one side of truth, we become fanatics, extremists.

The discernment of God's will is seldom easy. Always there will be some uncertainty, some risk of making a mistake. Almost all of us are forced to live with some uncertainty regarding God's will. This means that it is all right to make decisions even when there is a real risk of being in error. All that is expected of us is to use whatever tools available to arrive at the truth and then go ahead and act even when in doubt.

Some temperaments find this more difficult to do than others. Those who have a poor self-image or have a history of frequent mistakes have a much greater need of certainty than those who have a good self-image and a history of successes. At times we all need authority figures or objective friends who can help us make good decisions.

In the past we have been too simplistic in our supposition that those in authority have been given extraordinary gifts of discernment regarding the will of God. There is abundant evidence of countless errors and mistakes in judgment on the part of popes, bishops and other superiors. The Second Vatican Council admitted some of these errors thus acknowledging that those in authority are not totally protected from error as we have imagined. However, because of the need for unity and harmony in the world, the decisions of authorities need to be taken seriously.

On the other hand, those in authority should be sufficiently humble not to trust only their own insights but to seek advice and help from others, including those under their command. The Spirit of Truth is available to all of us, laity as well as clergy, and we need to be open to this presence of the Holy Spirit in the laity. It seems that the human race is being challenged at the present time to break away from the old, blind obedience to those in authority and to accept the risk of error. The example of the blind obedience of the German people to Hitler should help us take this risk.

There are some persons who are unable to make right decisions in the midst of the uncertainties of life. They need to depend upon the help of a trusted friend or institution. This is not the ideal towards which we should strive. Our trust in God's loving care should be sufficient to enable us to be at peace with our decision without absolute certainty.

The uncertainty regarding the accuracy of our discernment is very disturbing for many people. They desperately seek some sort of absolute certainty to reassure themselves and give them peace. If we wait for absolute certainty in our process of discernment, we would never be able to get out of bed in the morning, lest we slip and break our hip. All that God asks of us is that we do the best we can to arrive at the decision which will do the greatest good both for ourselves and others. We must not be afraid to make mistakes. They are a necessary part of life on earth. Even if we use all the help available to comprehend God's will, there will always be some uncertainty in our decision.

Since mistakes are inevitable, it is important that we be honest enough to admit our errors, once we are made aware of them. This awareness usually occurs when we see the bad results of our course of action. Other times we become convinced of our fault through the intervention of others. Therefore, we should always seriously consider the objections or disagreements which others express regarding our judgments. It does not mean that they are always right and we always wrong. If we are sufficiently humble, we will acknowledge the possibility of a mistake on our part and be open to a second opinion from others.

Discernment is something that we need to do all day long. It goes into the many decisions we make regarding what we shall do or say, how to spend our time, when or what to eat, when to go to bed, when to get up, which TV program to watch, what book to read, how to react to the words or actions of others, etc., etc. Naturally some of our decisions are much more important than others, but all our decisions have significance since they are based on the priorities we have chosen for our life and destiny.

The following general rules will help us make the right decision especially when it is a matter of importance.

1. Clarify what options you have, what possible choices face you.

2. Pray for light and guidance from God.

3. Gather all the relevant data needed.

4. Become aware of your prejudices, selfish attachments, hang-ups which may distract you from knowing and doing the right thing.

5. Seek help and advice from others, especially in important things.

6. Prayerfully weigh all the options using one or more of the fifteen methods suggested below.

Choose the option that seems most in accord with truth, justice, love, goodness, beauty, unity, balance, wholeness.

Fifteen Ways to Discern God's Will

1. Use common sense to decide what will do the most good for everyone.

2. Use the three commandments of love of God, others and self to discern what will best fulfill our responsibilities to God, others and self.

3. Make a list of all reasons for and against each possible option.

4. Take the problem to prayer and talk it over with God or Jesus.

5. Consult others whose judgment you trust.

6. Make a tentative decision and sleep on it for a few days, then repeat the process of the previous five ways.

7. Try to imagine what Jesus might do if he were here in your place.

8. Try to find an appropriate text in the Bible that applies to the present situation, e.g. a similar action in the life of Jesus.

9. If the situation is serious, ask God for a sign.

10. If possible, experiment with a tentative decision and check the results of one's action. "By their fruits you will know them."

11. In case of doubt, retain the status quo. The burden of proof is always on the new direction that one is considering.

12. If both choices seem equally good, do the thing one least wants to do, since we can presume that we are biased in our own favor.

13. If one is being challenged to accomplish something heroic, be sure to test the upper limits of one's endurance, then pull back a few steps. It is important that we keep a reserve of energy upon which to rebuild one's

strength, otherwise permanent harm may be done to oneself.

14. Draw straws or toss a coin if none of the above methods of discernment indicate God's will. The apostles did this (see Acts of Apostles 1:26).

15. Open the Bible at random and try to find an answer from the first text that meets the eyes. This should be used only as a last resort when all the other methods fail to bring about a decision.

Discerning God's Plan for the World

If we are to attain our divinely given destiny on earth, our first task is to make contact with God in order to discern what God had in mind when S/He chose to create us. The gift of Knowledge is the primary way that the Holy Spirit reveals to us God's plan for the human race and the world. The four Gospels will help us discover God's plan as revealed to us by Jesus. He tells us that he is the way, the truth and the life and that no one can come to the Father except through him (John 14:6). Our personal destiny is linked with the overall plan of God for the human race. Jesus calls this plan the Kingdom of God. By "Kingdom of God," Jesus meant that situation where God reigns and rules and we accept His total freedom to do whatever S/He wants to do with us. This Kingdom is accomplished in our lives to the extent that we put no obstacles to God's will for us.

It is God's will that the whole human race participate in this Kingdom. God wishes to make us co-heirs with Christ in sharing all the riches of God Himself. The New Testament assures us that ultimately God will bring about His Kingdom. This will be accomplished by God's intervention into the history of the world and into our individual lives. The prime example of such intervention was Incarnation of Jesus Christ. We speak of interventions in our personal life as special moments of divine grace. All of us have had such experiences.

Each of us has the power to change the course of history of the world by sending out waves of love, grace and mercy all over the world. We can either specify the persons we wish this energy of love to influence or simply send out waves of love in all directions and trust God to apply them to whomever is most in need of that love. With such love we can assist God in bringing about the Kingdom of God upon earth.

Signs of Spiritual Progress

While here on earth we will always live with uncertainty. Our trust in God's loving care must be sufficient to enable us to be at peace with a lack of absolute certitude in discerning God's will for us. However, as we mature, the development of certain personal attributes will give us confidence that we are discerning God's will correctly in our life. These signs of spiritual progress are listed below.

1. A growing awareness of *greater trust* in God. More often than any other teaching, Jesus insists on blind faith and trust in God. Faith and trust are the keys which unlock the infinite treasury of God's goodness.

2. A growing awareness of *humble submission* of our will to the will of God. As we grow in holiness there is less resistance to doing God's will.

3.   A growing awareness of *greater gratitude* to God. Gratitude is a positive way of practicing humility and counteracting pride and ego inflation.

4.   A growing awareness of *greater intimacy* with Jesus. This has been the experience of every Christian saint.

5.   An ever *greater desire and longing for God, for God's love and for holiness*. This desire should become so intense that it dominates all other desires. We want sanctity because this is what God wants for us.

6.   Our conscious mind becomes *more and more centered in God and the things of God* rather than in ourselves and our wants. The thought of God becomes more constantly present throughout the waking hours of each day.

7.   *Simplicity of lifestyle.* As we progress in holiness our desires for worldly goods and sensual pleasures become less and less. We become content to do with less of good things of earth rather than more and more.

8.   An ever greater experience of the *fruits of the Holy Spirit* (Gal. 5:22).

To be able to discern progress in any one of these areas of spiritual growth we need to compare our present situation with that of a year ago, or even three or five years ago. Such progress is usually slow and not to be seen from one day to the next. Progress is needed in all eight areas, but genuine progress in any one of them makes it easier to experience an advance in the others. At different times in our life God wills for us to work on first one and then another. By prayer we discern God's will.

REFLECTION AND DISCUSSION

1. What is pending in your life that requires discernment in order to move forward in growth and wholeness? Commit to a study of this chapter, and select the steps you think will work for you in this decision-making process of discerning the right course of action. Follow through and discipline yourself to listen for the prompts of the Holy Spirit as you discern your response and act on it.

2. How will the above process differ when applied to an experience of group/parish/family/community discernment?

CHAPTER 21

Our Vocation in the Communion of Saints

There is an infinite variety to the possibilities of our experiencing the Gifts and Fruits of the Holy Spirit. All those who, in one way or another, are united to the Holy Spirit, form a community of persons which is called the Communion of Saints. Whether these persons are in heaven, purgatory or on earth, they are bound by the closest of all ties – that of the Spirit of God. Just as the Holy Spirit of Love joins the Father and Son in the Blessed Trinity, this same Spirit unites the great brotherhood and sisterhood of Christians throughout the earth to the souls of the just in heaven and purgatory. The fellowship that we enjoy in the Communion of Saints is a two-way street. Through the Holy Spirit, we are able to help others and they, in turn, can help us. The more traffic there is between the different members of the family of God, the more quickly we will reach our consummation on the Last Day. The coming of God's Kingdom and the personal salvation of each member are the concern of all the other members. In the world of grace there is no place for rugged individualism or self-ishness. What we have received so generously from God through the Church, we must endeavor to share with our brethren. Gratitude to God and love for our fellow-travelers urge us to do everything possible to share with others the wonderful graces that have been given us.

Our work for souls should be intimately connected with the particular vocation we choose. Our apostolic endeavors were never meant to be a mere sideline, while our main effort was directed to pleasing ourselves and the world. Instead, we should study our talents and abilities and determine how we can best use them to further the Kingdom of God upon earth. There are many tasks that need to be performed in order to bring to completion the Communion of Saints. We need the institution of Marriage to generate the love and the people who will complete the number of the elect. We need to eat, sleep, travel, be clothed, warmed and protected, as well as baptized, confirmed, forgiven and nourished with the Sacraments. God has generously bestowed upon mankind a variety of gifts and interests, so that all the needs of the human family will be fulfilled. It is the duty of each of us to find the particular way that we can best help our brethren. Whenever we discover our proper vocation, we will find a deep satisfaction in doing well the things for which we were created.

It is not easy to determine the particular work we should do in life. To add to the difficulties, we live in an age where the majority of people have distorted ideas about the purpose of work. How many people realize that its primary purpose is to serve God and our fellow man? We do not merely work in order to live, but rather we should live so that we can work and help others to attain the fullness of life, both natural and supernatural. Work is not a curse imposed by God upon mankind; it is only the burden of sweat and toil that was added to the original command to "till and keep" the garden (Gn 2:15). Instead of trying to escape work by finding the job with the most pay and the least effort, our attitude should be that of Christ and the heavenly Father: "My Father works even until now and I work" (Jn 5:17). If we are normal and healthy and if we have found the tasks for which we are best suited, all of us should find great joy and satisfaction in our work.

When our educators properly fulfill their assigned tasks, the average person is ready to choose his vocation at the beginning of adulthood. The young adult should consult older and wiser persons before deciding upon one's life's work. The Holy Spirit should also be consulted through prayer and meditation upon the Kingdom of God and its needs. Then, after proper deliberation, a choice should be made and preparation should begin for it. Ordinarily, there should be no looking back or continued searching for greener fields. If a mistake has been made, divine providence will indicate clearly what we should do. Presuming that one has made a sincere effort to discover God's will, it is essential for one's peace of mind that we believe the Lord will not abandon us. Even if we make a mistake, the Lord is able to arrange things, so that there will be abundant opportunity to do our part in completing the Kingdom of God. "For those who love God, all things work together unto good" (Rom 8:28).

As far as possible, we should live in the present, without too much concern about the past or the future. We should take each day as it is given us and with the time and energy available, do everything possible to be of service to God and others. For most of us, there will always be more tasks to do than we have the time or ability. We should try to choose the more important; do them well and let the others go undone. We will eventually discover that these other tasks were either not important or that someone else did them. In our choice of the work to be done, we must observe the proper order of love. Those with the greatest need merit our first attention; and if there are several with the same need, we choose the one who has the first right to our love.

We will often make mistakes in judgment, but this is not important, provided we are sincere and generous in what we do. We must give and give and give, without counting the cost. Having received so much, it is now our vocation to share these good things with others. We should not demand that they appreciate what we are doing for them, since our purpose is to show appreciation for what God and others have already given us. Realizing that we have but a few years to spend upon earth, we should be determined to do as much good as we can with the resources available. We take up where our brethren of a former generation had to stop; we simply carry on the work of creation and salvation another step. When we grow old or die, we can hope that God will provide others to carry his Kingdom a further step toward completion. The burden of the whole world does not depend upon any one of us. Each of us is needed for the particular contribution that divine destiny has planned for us. Some are asked to give more than others, but we should all be as generous as we possibly can. Like Christ, we must spend our time, "going about doing good" (Acts 10:38). "I must do the works of him who sent me while it is day; night is coming when no one can work" (Jn 9:4).

In our efforts to help others, we must learn to work as a team with others and not try to do our job alone. First of all, we need the advice of those wiser and more experienced than ourselves. We need friends and perhaps the greatest of all our friends will be the spiritual director, who guides us in making the decisions needed to attain maturity and sanctity. God has shared his gifts with many people and there is so much to be done that we must find a place for every person who is willing to work. Not only must we give help to others; we must allow them to aid us in our needs. It is not charity for us always to be giving and never receiving. Very often the greatest favor we can do for a person is to give him the opportunity to be useful and to make a worthwhile contribution to our own happiness as well as to the happiness of others.

God had very good reason for creating us weak and in need of help from each other. This serves to keep us humble and encourages our friends to exercise their charity toward us. Realizing our great needs, we should turn without hesitation to the other members of the Communion of Saints and beg humbly for their help. Our salvation often depends upon these brethren of ours. Only after death shall we realize how much we owe to the prayers of the saints and angels in heaven and the souls in purgatory. As to the help we receive from the Communion of Saints on earth, all of us realize how greatly dependent is our salvation upon our parents, teachers, directors, superiors and other spiritual friends. If God had so chosen, he could have created some other dispensation of grace in which we would have received our salvation directly from the Lord. There are some people who, in proud independence, would like to think that this is still the way to be saved. Despite what they may think, it is through the Community of God's people that we receive the necessary grace.

At the head of the Communion of Saints is Jesus Christ, the God-Man. He is the mediator of the new covenant of love under which all of us have been born and will be saved. Instead of standing alone, Christ has willed to include our efforts and sacrifices in the total work of redemption. "I rejoice in the sufferings I bear for your sake, and what is lacking of the sufferings of Christ, I fill up in my flesh for his body, which is the Church" (Col 1:24). Through this sharing of his work, our Lord has made an admirable contribution to the bonds of love that unite the members of the family of God. If we never had to depend upon this family, nor they upon us, we would forget one another. By establishing this constant communication of mutual aid between the different parts of the Community, love is greatly fostered. We become grateful for the wonderful household of saints to which we belong and we resolve to become involved in all its activities. Because of the greatness of their love, some members deserve our attention more than others. Like a little child turning to a big brother or an elder sister, we should go without hesitation to the great saints to seek their help in time of need.

REFLECTION AND DISCUSSION

1. How does God act through you in the work you do? What helps you to experience God's presence as you work with others?

2. When there is disharmony or dissension among co-workers, what acts of practical, peace-making love can change the tone?

CHAPTER 22

The Faith of the Blessed Virgin Mary

The saint closest to Christ in every way is Mary, the Blessed Mother. As the brethren of Christ, all of us are related to Mary most intimately. Being the eldest daughter of the Church, Mary is our "big sister" who is so much wiser, better and more experienced than we are. As the mother of Jesus, she is the mother of that life of Christ that dwells within everyone who is in the state of grace. In addition to all this, we are related to Mary as members of the same human family. It is through her that the whole human race is related by flesh and blood to the Son of God. It was a piece of her human flesh that became the divine flesh of the God-Man and it was the humanity received from her that paid the price of our redemption on Good Friday, arose gloriously and immortal on Easter Sunday, ascended triumphantly on Ascension Thursday, and that now sits at the right hand of God in heaven, equal to the heavenly Father in all things.

Jesus Christ will always be the perfect model of sanctity for all Christians. Before the Incarnation, Mary was the first example for the human race, but once Christ was conceived, he became the supreme representative of all mankind. Mary in her willing holiness is our supreme model at the Incarnation, on Calvary, at Pentecost, today in heaven and during the Mass. In each of these mysteries of our redemption, Mary plays a secondary role to that of Christ, but nevertheless, an essential role. In the particular plan of salvation chosen by God, her activity is necessary if the plan is to reach a successful conclusion. The Incarnation of Christ depends upon the free consent of Mary. It would be contrary to all nature and reason for God to have compelled Mary, against her will, to be the mother of Christ. What would have happened if she had said "no" we can only conjecture, but we can presume that God would have found another way to save us. Thanks be to God, Mary said "Yes" and for this we should always be grateful.

The activity of Mary in the work of Christ's redemption centers on her faith and love. At the Incarnation, she was asked to consent to his life; on Calvary, she had to consent to his death. Actually, the two consents were but one act of loving faith, since her blind assent to God's will at the Annunciation carried with it a virtual consent to the whole work of salvation. Like Mary, we also have to work in the darkness of faith throughout our life on earth. Therefore, a study of how she acted in times of crisis will help us to make the right decisions when our faith and love are put to the test. If we will consent wholeheartedly to each of God's calls of grace, as did Mary at the Annunciation, we too will experience an incarnation of the life of Christ within us. If we accept our role of suffering as Mary accepted her pain on Calvary, we will have a share in Christ's work of redemption. The following verse from Colossians describes what is ours to give: "What is lacking of the sufferings of Christ I fill up in my flesh for his body, which is the Church" (Col 1:24).

The first crisis of which we are aware in the life of Mary occurred at the Annunciation. "When she heard (the

Angel) she was troubled at his word and kept pondering what manner of greeting this might be" (Lk 1:29). "How shall this happen, since I do not know man?" (Lk 1:34). Having been told what God wanted of her, it still required an heroic act of faith on her part to make the plunge into the vast, unknown territory of divine motherhood. Nevertheless, she wholeheartedly accepted everything that God willed for her. "Behold the handmaid of the Lord, be it done to me according to thy word" (Lk 1:38). At this crucial moment in the history of salvation, it is Mary's act of faith that wins the victory over Satan and sin. "Blessed is she who has believed, because the things promised her by the Lord shall be accomplished" (Lk 1:45). In abandoning herself completely to God, Mary's faith and love took a tremendous step forward; the capacity of her soul for grace was enlarged and the Lord filled it to overflowing. Having received so much from the Lord, her first thought is to share it with others. Being filled herself with Christ, she gives him to others whenever she gives herself. "How have I deserved that the mother of my Lord should come to me," St. Elizabeth asked at the time of the Visitation (Lk 1:43). As Mary brought the invisible Christ to Elizabeth and Zachary, she was vividly aware of her own lowliness, along with the greatness of her new vocation. "My soul magnifies the Lord and my spirit rejoices in God my Savior; because he has regarded the lowliness of his handmaid; for behold, henceforth all generations shall call me blessed; because he who is mighty has done great things for me and holy is his name" (Lk 1:46-49). Following her example, we must allow ourselves to be so filled with Christ that we, too, will become Christ-bearers.

Christian tradition insists that Mary was the virginal mother of Christ. She shared in the work of redemption through the acts of faith, which were required of her during the nativity and infancy of Christ. Again and again she had to make acts of blind faith in the Word of God that gave testimony to his divinity. Each time her faith was tested, she responded wholeheartedly to God's grace.

At the Presentation, Simeon made plain to her two facts: (1) "This child is destined for the fall and the rise of many in Israel and for a sign that shall be contradicted; (2) thy own soul a sword shall pierce" (Lk 2:34-35). Still living in the darkness of faith, she did not know all that this might entail, but it was clear that there would be much suffering. Pain is contrary to our human nature and no mother could naturally desire this vocation for either her child or herself. St. Luke says that Mary and Joseph were astonished at what they heard, but there was no refusal to accept God's will. Making the necessary effort, Mary rose above the desires of her natural motherhood and made a new step of faith into the unknown future.

Another act of faith was required when they found the Christ-child in the temple. "They did not understand the word that he spoke to them" (Lk 2:50). Again, working in the dark, Mary conformed her will to the will of God. Her natural motherly possessiveness of Jesus had to be made subservient to his "Father's business" (Lk 2:49). We can only guess at the effort required to rise to this new relationship. This would not be the only time that Christ would ask her to take a place second to others. At Cana she is told, "What is this to me and to you, my hour has not yet come" (Jn 2:4). During his public life, our Lord makes answer to the woman who praised his mother, "Rather, blessed are they who hear the word of God and keep it" (Lk 11:28). Once she tried to interrupt him during a busy day with the disciples. "Behold, thy mother and thy brethren are outside, seeking thee." Jesus answered, "Who are my mother and my brethren?" And stretching forth his hands toward his disciples, he said, "Behold my mother and my brethren" (Mt 12:47-49). Mary humbly submitted to her secondary role during the public life of Christ. She had no claims upon him when it was a matter of his proclaiming the good news of salvation. Because she was willing to follow God's will, Mary has become the model of all those, especially mothers, who must sacrifice their natural possessiveness on one level in order to rise to a new height of maturity and sanctity. "His mother kept all these things carefully in her heart" (Lk 2:51).

Mary's vocation was that of a mother, not an apostle. She is not given the commission to go out and preach the Gospel to all nations. Nevertheless, she can help all those who are called to be apostles. Her vocation is truly motherly; it is an interior mission of prayer and suffering. She is not permitted near Christ during the public life of preaching, but we find her very close to him at the two key moments of his life on earth – his incarnation and his death. At the conception and birth of Christ, she is to the God-Man everything a mother is supposed to be. On Calvary, through her union with Christ in his sufferings, she offers to the heavenly Father her faith and hope, her love as a mother and a woman, and unites these to the supreme offering of love made by Christ. Each time that the Sacrifice of Calvary is renewed in the

Mass, these elements of Mary's sacrifice are integrated into Christ's and our sacrifice.

As Christ's mother, she willingly offered her Son on Calvary for the redemption of the world. Just as this was the crowning act of love on the part of Christ, so it was the greatest of all the acts of faith, hope and charity which Mary was ever asked to make. By cooperating with Jesus in the salvation of the world, she acquired a new title as mother of mankind. Christ is the new Adam and Mary becomes the new Eve of the redeemed human race. Mary's spiritual motherhood of all those who belong to Christ is a type of that supernatural motherhood which the Church, the Mystical Body of Christ, enjoys over us. The Church began only with the death of Christ; therefore, Mary anticipates the Church. At the Annunciation and on Calvary, the Church was hidden in Mary. She experienced in advance all that the new people of God would experience later.

On Pentecost, Mary once again assumes the hidden role Christ asked her to accept during his public life. She remains in the background, humbly subject to the authority of Christ in St. Peter and the Apostles, just as she had submitted herself earlier to her Son. However, this does not mean that she is no longer needed for the work of the Church. Mary still has the very important motherly task of praying for the Church, especially all those active in the apostolate. During the remaining years of her earthly life and throughout the centuries since her Assumption, Mary's vocation is primarily that of intercessor before the throne of the heavenly Father. She is not alone today; the first Pentecost is re-enacted as the whole communion of Saints unites its prayers with hers and with Christ's for a new Pentecost, a new day of grace. "All these with one mind continued steadfastly in prayer with the women and Mary, the Mother of Jesus, and with his brethren" (Acts 1:14).

By her Assumption, Mary has become the fulfillment of all that the Church ever hopes to attain. Her life of faith while on earth is a perfect model for our faith; likewise, her glorified body in heaven gives added reason to our own hope of resurrection. Beside the assurance of the Risen Body of Christ, we are given a further incentive to our hope for the third aeon in the doctrine of the Assumption. What has happened to the body of Mary will also occur for us, if we have followed her example of heroic faith, hope and charity. The glorification of her body takes our faith another step toward completion, since we are concerned here with a human person and not a divine Person. There can be no doubt that God intends to glorify us just as he glorified Jesus, the God-Man, and Mary, the first member of Christ's Church.

Meditation on the mysteries of our salvation as seen in Mary, can be a most fruitful source for our growth in grace. If we understand her vocation as the Mother of God, devotion to Mary will never lead us away from Christ but always to a closer union with him. She is in no way above him or equal to him, but rather totally subservient to him. Her one desire for us in relation to her divine Son is expressed with beautiful simplicity in the words she spoke to the servants at Cana, "Do whatever he tells you" (Jn 2:5). Her power of intercession and mediation, like the whole Communion of Saints, has value only in and through Christ. "There is one God and one Mediator between God and men, himself man, Christ Jesus" (1Tim 2:5). She is not a second Christ, she is the mother of Christ, and all her value to the world and to God is found in her motherhood, both natural and spiritual. Because her vocation as mother is so similar to our vocation as a creature, we do well to learn all we can about her, ask her intercession, and imitate her faith, hope and charity.

We do all the above each time we recite the rosary and meditate on the twenty mysteries. Each time we recite the Hail Mary, we ask Mary to pray for us at the two most important moments of our life: now, this present moment, and the moment of our death. For those of us who have frequently recited the rosary during our life on earth, what a consolation it will be, as we approach our death, to know how many hundreds and thousands of times during our life we have asked Mary to pray for us at that moment.

REFLECTION AND DISCUSSION

1. Imagine you and Mary are visiting together. What would you like to ask her?

2. Mary held fast in her love of Jesus even to his death by crucifixion. At that moment, his life must have seemed to be a failure, yet she stood by and offered the comfort of her presence even when she could not alter the circumstances. Think of a time in your life when someone you hold dear has experienced a failure. Consider how your fidelity, even in the face of failure, can be a transforming event in the life of this person.

CHAPTER 23

The Heroic Charity of the Saints

Besides the Blessed Mother, everyone should have his or her favorite saints from both sexes. Frequently one will find in a saint of the opposite sex the necessary complement to one's own personality. Getting to know this saint quite well will enable one to grow in natural maturity as well as sanctity. By studying the saint's life and especially his or her words, we can get to know the personality well enough to feel a truly intimate friendship for someone long since dead. It is important that we read those lives of the saints that are honestly written, giving both sides of the saint's temperament and character. Simply because the Church has canonized them does not mean they were always saints. Nearly all of them had evil tendencies that required great grace and heroic efforts on their part to transform into virtues. If we get a true picture of their struggle to attain sanctity, we receive immense consolation and encouragement in our own efforts and failures.

Every person is unique in the particular character and vocation given by God; therefore, it is a grave error to attempt a slavish imitation of any one of the saints. The only exception to this is our imitation of Jesus Christ who, as the God-Man, completely comprehends all the possible types of personality and sanctity that may be created. An attempt to pattern our lives exactly after that of a saint is especially dangerous if we do not have a clear and complete picture of that person. Even when the biographies or autobiographies are adequate and true, it is wrong to accept what they did as being also best for us. Religious should know the particular spirit of the founder of their order or congregation and try to maintain this same spirit. However, it is a mistake when religious try to follow their founder in every word and detail of his or her life.

For one thing, times and conditions have changed. It is reasonable to suppose that if the particular founder or foundress were living today, he or she would often act differently from what was done in another age. The world has advanced tremendously in the knowledge of revealed truth as well as nature. Simply because a man or woman was a great saint does not mean that this person made no mistakes during life. It is necessary that we subject each of the words and actions of the saint to the principles of right reason, as we know them today. If they appear valid, we should follow them. This is the way that we follow our friends on earth. Because we love someone very dearly does not make that person infallible. Only a childish, immature love is blind to the faults of the beloved. In our relationship with the great saints of the past, we must love and accept them in a mature way.

There is one area of their life where we can imitate the saints without hesitation and this is their love for God, their neighbors and themselves. We ought to study the heroic charity that these great friends of God achieved, so that we can gain inspiration and enlightenment for our own lives. Each of them developed this field of charity in a unique way, according to the specific vocation and personality given to them. By studying the manner in which these saints practiced charity, we will know better what God expects of us. We should try to find saints who had similar vocations to our own; likewise those who have lived near our time or in similar conditions of life. When we find a personality and temperament that strikes a responsive chord in our souls, then we have discovered a true friend in the full sense of the word.

In each of the saints we can discover a special charm. Besides their great charity, the thing most appealing in the saints is their simplicity. They are so honest and straightforward: free of masks and completely themselves. Because they were so open in their speech and manner of behavior, they usually made enemies who resented their directness. It makes interesting reading to see how the saints coped with their persecutors, either before or after their death. A delightful sense of humor will often be seen in the saints who refused to take themselves too seriously and also in the way our Lord dealt with those who opposed them. We all appreciate genuineness and sincerity and these qualities will never be lacking in any saint. Their life is a straight line toward God, without any double-dealing or complexities. This simplicity will be noticed especially in their prayer life. They realized that God was a real person, someone to whom they could speak directly and from the heart.

Their heroic charity gave them a familiarity and confidence with the Lord that served as a recompense for the many crosses they endured to attain sanctity. Although keenly aware of their own weakness and nothingness, they were very much aware of God's infinite goodness and deep love for them. Their humility and confidence in God gave a beautiful balance to their lives that enabled them to run swiftly along the path of holiness. Filled with great faith and hope, the saints were able to attain a wonderful peace and joy here upon earth. They vividly realized that God is all-powerful, all-wise and all-good. They had many proofs of God's infinite love for them. Putting all these ingredients together, they discovered a recipe for happiness right here in the second aeon. All of this reflected in their faces, their eyes, their smile, their entire behavior. Most of all, it is seen in the serene confidence they have toward the future as well as the present. Those who are close to them will imbibe some of this same confidence, if they are open to God's grace. God proportions his goodness to the degree of our confidence in him. "If thou canst believe, all things are possible to those who believe" (Mk 9:23).

Another characteristic of the charity of the saints is seen in the immense desires they have. There is nothing small about anything they do, whether it is motivated by natural love or supernatural charity. They are never content with the lowest place in God's esteem, even though keenly aware of how little they deserve his love. Love has made them bold and daring in their desires. They have come to realize that he never resents these high aspirations, but takes great delight in giving his love in proportion to one's desires. They know that we can never ask too much of God; that we actually show honor to his infinity when we make these bold requests. Neither does the consciousness of their past sins hinder their high desires. They know that God's love is sufficient to take away all their sins as a drop of water might disappear in a flaming furnace.

The saint is not content merely to ask for great things for herself; she is just as desirous that these same things

be shared by all her brethren. She has a deep consciousness of the needs of the whole human family – their
problems become her problems. Love and sanctity are
actually synonymous. Therefore, for the saint, love of
God and brethren are as natural and instinctive as
breathing. They have, in a real sense, become all love,
loving without measure or limit, loving even unto folly.
In the eyes of many of their friends, they may appear
foolish and impractical in the extremes to which their
love will go. Without concern for human respect, they
desire to love God and all of God's family, as they have
never been loved in the past. They endeavor to let no
opportunity pass, no matter how small, when it is possible for them to be of service to God and others.

The heroic charity of the saints will be expressed by a
great zeal for God's glory and for the spread of his
Kingdom. Aflame with his love, they are never happy
unless working in some way for his glory and the welfare of their neighbors. They tax their minds and imagi-
nations to discover all the possible ways to carry out
their great charity. Following the example of Christ
when he washed the feet of the apostles, their whole life
is one of humble service to their brethren, being willing
to lay down their lives for the salvation of others. They
desire God to be known, loved and served by all and
they do all in their power to tell the world about the
wonderful things of God. They suffer keenly when they
see God's love despised, ignored or rejected. They are
ever seeking generous souls who will give to God the
love that he deserves and desires. "We have but the one
day of this life to save them, and so give to Our Lord a proof
of our love. To-morrow will be Eternity, then Jesus will reward you a hundredfold for the sweet joys you have given up

for Him." (St. Therese, *Letters to Her Brother Mission-aries*). Believing that love makes all things possible, the saints are never discouraged by their own weakness and smallness. Through faith and hope, they know that even their highest desires can be accomplished.

Charity, like faith and hope, is a supernatural gift of God. In order to receive so great a love, the saint must abandon her whole self to God. The writings of the saints find different ways to describe this complete surrender of their being to the love of God. It is sometimes called the "gift of oneself" to emphasize the freedom of choice that the saint offers in making available for God's use all the faculties and energies that have been given her. They may speak of themselves as victims of love, to express the total consecration of their life to God. Victimhood means that their gift of self is absolute, indeterminate, everlasting, constantly renewed and completely generous. This is sometimes expressed as abandonment to the will of God, to emphasize that they allow God to dispose of them as he chooses. They have endeavored to make their wills so completely attuned to the least inspiration of grace, that they respond instantly to every indication of God's will for them, and joyfully accept it, no matter how lowly or difficult may be the task assigned to them. If God so wills, they accept without hesitation the heaviest crosses, suffering intensely but patiently as did Christ, their model. That no conditions have been placed on their surrender is proven by the selflessness of their lives. Their dedication to God is prudent, calm, humble, trustful, entire, courageous, persevering.

An interesting thing about the great saints is that it is often difficult to determine the particular temperament that was most natural to them. As a person grows toward the fullness of sanctity, he learns to develop all the unconscious powers of his character. Through cooperation with God's grace, the saint has succeeded in bringing to perfection all the different sides of his personality originally asleep in the depths of his soul. Just as in our Lord's life, we can see every possible temperament perfectly portrayed, so in a similar way we see a beautiful balance in the personality of the heroic saint. On different occasions, he will show forth first one virtue and them another; but all of them are fused by charity into a marvelous simplicity. This is the peace possessed by the saints.

At the same time, there is a wonderful variety among the saints. Each of them has developed his particular talents and personality to perfection and no two of them are alike. For this reason, we find ourselves attracted at times more to one saint than to another. Often in our devotion, we pass from one saint to another; a saint that was a great inspiration to us in youth will not necessarily be the model we follow in mature adulthood. Divine providence has mercifully given us this almost unlimited choice, so that there will be a saint for every occasion. If we come to know them well, we will find in their example the inspiration to help us attain the particular manifestation of heroic charity that God desires for us. If God were willing to help them reach the heights of love that they did, we can believe and hope that he will do the same for us.

REFLECTION AND DISCUSSION

1. Consider your special community of saints. Some may be canonized and/or admired throughout the world. Others may be deceased friends or members of your family. Write a dialogue between one of your saints and yourself, inviting God's Spirit of wisdom into the process. Tell them how much their earthly life means to you. Talk with them about your burdens, your joys. What will they answer? Take time for silence before you begin writing down their responses.

2. Consider ways in which you interact with the community of saints, both living and dead, canonized and not canonized, which we celebrate as Catholics. What interaction do you value the most?

CHAPTER 24

Third Aeon – Goal of Divine Love

All love looks forward with eager longing to a permanent union with the beloved. God's supernatural love desires not only that blessed union with our souls in heaven which we call the beatific vision; God also desires to be united with our whole nature, body and soul. This will be accomplished on the Last Day when we experience resurrection and share in the same union of love as the souls of the blessed now enjoy. To emphasize the very distinctive character of this new life which we will receive at the final coming of Christ, we call it the *Third Aeon*. The first aeon extended from the creation until the Incarnation of Jesus on earth. The second aeon began with the resurrection of Jesus and continues until the final coming of Jesus at the end of time. The third aeon will begin with the renewed creation of the Last Day and will continue forever. It will be the fulfillment of the Kingdom of God as promised by Jesus in the Gospels.

In the third aeon we will celebrate the glorious marriage of God and humanity which was the purpose of every one of God's acts of benevolence toward us. It will be here in this Kingdom of the Last Day that we will see in all its glory what God has had in mind for us from all eternity. At last we will understand what love is and what it can do, when it is God who does the loving. Without any fears of going to excess or any danger of abuse, we will be able to exercise all our desires of love to our heart's content. At every step of the way in the second aeon of our present life we are faced with new crises and conflicts. This phase of proving our love will end with the final coming of Christ. No more will we prefer humanity to God, ourselves to others. The perfect order of loving will have been permanently established, never again to be broken. Without any possible chance of going to extremes, we will be able to give free rein to every desire of love. Not only will we be given the grace to love God with an unlimited love; we will be able to exercise to the fullest all our powers of love toward each of our friends whom we have loved while upon earth. Now in our present aeon, we have to be careful with our love, lest we abuse it by going to excess or misdirecting it towards a creature to the exclusion of God. With the final coming of Christ, all these dangers will disappear, and we will be able to occupy ourselves entirely with loving all persons, both divine and created. "Behold I make all things new ... To him who thirsts I will give of the fountain of the water of life freely ... I will be your God and you shall be my child" (Rev 21:5-7).

With the final coming of Christ, evil will be banished forever. No longer will it be possible to be tempted or to sin. All the powerful forces of evil will have been decisively conquered. Besides moral and spiritual evil, all physical pain and suffering will likewise be removed. The darkness of error and ignorance will never again be allowed to overshadow us. The bright sun of truth will shed its light for all to see. By the light of this New Day we shall know all truth, all wisdom, all love. We shall know God as S/He knows us. No longer will there be any secrets among the beloved who have joined themselves irrevocably to Christ. We shall know everything we want to know about our friends and we shall be able at last to reveal our whole being to those we love. "The city has no need of the sun or the moon to shine upon it. For the glory of God lights it up and the Lamb is the lamp thereof. The nations shall walk by its light. The kings of the earth shall bring their glory and honor into it. Its gates shall not be shut by day, for there shall be no night. There shall not enter into it anything defiled" (Rev 21:23-27).

Here upon earth, in our present vale of tears, every love and joy is clouded by the fact of death. No matter how happy we are, we know that the joy will soon end to be replaced by new crosses, trials and afflictions. Worst of all, the presence of death is a fact we are never allowed to forget. No matter how full is our love and happiness in this present aeon, the fact of physical death always faces us and the danger of a second death of mortal sin is ever-present. In the third aeon, the possibility of both these deaths shall disappear. The skies above the New Jerusalem will always be bright, without a single storm cloud to mar a perfect day. "God will wipe away every tear from their eyes. Death shall be no more; neither shall there be mourning nor crying nor pain any more. For the former things have passed away" (Rev 21:4).

In our present way of life it is possible for us to enjoy three different relationships of love: love of parents, friends and spouse. These human relationships were given to us to prepare us for three similar forms of love with the three Persons of the Blessed Trinity. By means of grace-life we are able here and now to experience the love of a heavenly Parent, a divine Friend, Jesus Christ, and a spiritual spouse, the Holy Spirit. To the extent that we can enjoy these three relationships of love on earth, the Kingdom of God has already come for us. Nevertheless, it is always a blind and uncertain union of love on earth. We accept it on faith and are grateful for the possession of it, even though we are aware of how easily we can lose it. All of this will be changed with the final coming of Christ when the veil of faith will be removed forever. We will then be able to enjoy in all their fullness these three supernatural relationships of love which we have received through sanctifying grace. God will reveal the divine Parenthood of Mother and Father in all its glory. Jesus Christ will show himself to us both as a friend and a spouse. The Holy Spirit will be seen as the bond of love which unites us to God and to each other forever. "'Come, I will show you the bride, the spouse of the Lamb.' And he took me up in spirit to a mountain, great and high, and showed me the holy city Jerusalem, coming down out of heaven from God, having the glory of God. Its light was like a precious stone, as it were a jasper stone, clear as crystal" (Rev 21:10-11).

The glorious Kingdom of God upon earth began with the Incarnation of Jesus Christ in the womb of Mary. Beginning with this first marriage of God and human nature, the work of incarnation has spread throughout the world by means of grace. The resurrected body of Christ was the first piece of the completed Kingdom of the third aeon. By studying the eleven appearances of this glorified body of Jesus, we can learn much about the state of our own glorified bodies on the Last Day. The glorified Christ is now hidden in the clouds of heaven, seated at the right hand of the Father. At the end of time the clouds will open and we shall see the Body of Christ coming to resurrect our bodies and to unite us, body and soul, to God. Then will take place in the renewed creation that eternal wedding banquet about which our Lord speaks so often in the Gospels. "Let us be glad and rejoice, and give glory to him, for the marriage of the Lamb has come and his spouse has prepared herself ... Blessed are they who are called to the marriage supper of the Lamb" (Rev 19:7-9).

The doctrine of the future life in God's Kingdom is one of the most important revelations in the whole Bible. We should meditate often upon the passages of both Testaments which speak of this heavenly life. If interpreted according to this future dimension, everything in the words and actions of Jesus tell us something about the fullness of the Kingdom that will be established on the Last Day. Like the early Christians, we should become so fascinated by the third aeon that we will look forward to it with eager longing. Christianity is primarily a religion of the present and the future, not of the past. It is a religion of triumph and joy, not primarily of suffering and death. The glorified body of Jesus should dominate our thoughts much more than the passion and death of Jesus on Good Friday. During this second aeon it is necessary that we keep a balance between the cross and the resurrection, but we must never forget that suffering and death are only temporary means to an everlasting end: the glorious, eternal goal of the third aeon. If we allow ourselves to become truly enthused over this wonderful New Day that awaits us and the whole world, we will be willing to pay the necessary price to grow constantly in grace-life now in our present second aeon.

In the glorified life of the Last Day, God's love will reach its ultimate perfection and the last and greatest of the "New Days" will dawn upon the universe. A new heaven and a new earth will rise from the old to become the home of all those who have chosen to make a return of love to God's repeated calls of grace. All those who have learned to love, both naturally and supernaturally, will find a place in this third aeon. The time of testing will be over, for all eternity we will be able to enjoy the fruits of the efforts of the second aeon. Never again will we have to struggle and no longer will the outcome of our actions be in doubt. Our final decision for God and for love will have been made; an eternity of peace and happiness will stretch before us.

REFLECTION AND DISCUSSION

1. What do you consider as your personal work in furthering the Kingdom of God on earth? How are you hastening the coming of God's reign of divine love? Are there some ways in which you are hampering the expressing of God's grace among the people you encounter every day?

2. Imagine your community of faith giving full, unbridled expression to the joy God promises in the third aeon. How would your community be different?

SUGGESTED FURTHER READINGS

Anonymous :   *Cloud of Unknowing*, Paulist Press 1988.

                     The Way of the Pilgrim, Dover Publications
                     2003.

Augustine of   *City of God*, Random House 2000.
Hippo:

Berry, Thomas: *Dream of the Earth*, Sierra Club/University
                     of California Press 1988.

Irene de   *Knowing Woman*, Shambhala Publications
Castillejo: 1997.

Coleman,   *Whispers of Revelation*, Twenty-third
Bill & Patty: Publications 1992.

Jean-Pierre de   *Abandonment to Divine Providence*,
Caussade: Random House 1993.

DeMello, An-   *Wellsprings*, Image Books 1986.
thony: *Sadhana*, Image Books 1984.

Douglas, James: *The Non-violent Coming of God*, Orbis 1991.

Eadie, Betty: *Embraced by the Light*, Gold Leaf Press 1992.

                     The Awakening Heart, Pocket Books 1996.

Eisler, Riane: *The Chalice and the Blade*, 1st Harper & Row
                     1998.

Fischer,   *Women at the Well*, Paulist Press 1986.
Kathleen:

Foster, Richard: *Celebration of Discipline*, HarperCollins
                     2002.

                     Freedom of Simplicity, HarperCollins 1998.

                     The Challenge of a Disciplined Life, Harper-

Collins 1989.

Fox, Matthew:	*Original Blessing,* Bear & Company 1983.
Francis de Sales:	*Introduction to the Devout Life,* TAN Books 2009.
	Love of God, TAN Books 2009.
Frankl, Viktor:	*Man's Search for Meaning,* Rider & Company 2008.
Goerres, Ida:	*The Hidden Face,* Pantheon 1959.
Goodier, Alban:	*The Public Life of Our Lord Jesus Christ,* Vol 1-2, P. J. Kennedy & Sons 1937.
Green, Thomas:	*A Vacation With the Lord,* Ignatius Press 2000.
	When the Well Runs Dry, Ave Maria Press 1995.
	Drinking From the Dry Well, Ave Maria Press 1995.
Guenther, Margaret:	*Holy Listening,* Darton Longman & Todd Ltd 1992.
Guardini, Romano:	*The Lord,* Gateway Publishers 1982.
Hurnard, Hannah:	*Hinds Feet in High Places*, Destiny Image 2005.
Johnson, Robert:	*HE,* Harper & Row 1989.
	SHE, Harper & Row 1977.
	WE, HarperCollins 1983.
Kelsey, Morton:	*Encounter with God,* Bethany House 1975.
	Christianity as Psychology, Augsburg Fortress 1986.
	The Other Side of Silence, Paulist Press 1997.
	God, Dreams, and Revelation, Augsburg Fortress 1991.
	Companions on the Inner Way, Crossroads Publishing 1996.

Kunkel, Fritz:	*Creation Continues,* Word Inc. 1973.
Lawrence, Brother:	*The Practice of the Presence of God,* Paraclete Press 2010.
Leonard, Linda:	*The Wounded Woman,* Shambhala 1982.
Linn M & D:	*Healing the Eight Stages of Life,* Paulist Press 1988.
May, Gerald:	*Care of Mind, Care of Spirit,* Harper & Row 1982.
	Addiction and Grace, HarperOne 2007
McNutt, Francis:	*Healing,* Ave Maria Press 1999.
Merton, Thomas:	*Contemplative Prayer,* Image 1971.
	Conjectures of a Guilty Bystander, Image 1968.
	Seeds of Contemplation, New Directions 1998.
Michael, Chester & Norrisey, Marie	*Prayer and Temperament,* Open Door 1985.
	Arise, Open Door 1985.
Michael, Chester:	*Beatitudes,* Open Door 1990.
	The Four Steps of Individuation, Open Door 1997.
	The Different Levels of Faith, Open Door 1988.
	Discernment, Open Door 1992.
	Different World Views, Open Door 1996.
	A Balanced Christianity, Open Door 1981.
Miller, William:	*Make Friends With Your Shadow,* Augsburg Fortress 1981.
	Your Golden Shadow, Harper & Row 1989.
Nouwen, Henri:	*Reading Out,* Image 1986.
	The Road to Daybreak, Image 1990.
	With Burning Hearts, Orbis Books 2003.
Peck, Scott:	*The Road Less Traveled,* Touchstone Books 1998.
	People of the Lie, Arrow 1990.
Pennington, Basil:	*Centering Prayer,* Image 1982.
	Centered Living, Liguori Publications 1999.

Roberts, Bernadette:	*The Path to No-Self,* State University of New York 1991.
	The Experience of No-Self, Shambhala 1981.
Sanford, John:	*The Invisible Partner,* Paulist Press 1980.
	The Kingdom Within, HarperOne 1987.
	Healing and Wholeness, Paulist Press 1977.
	Dreams: God's Forgotten Language, HarperOne 1989.
Savary, L.; Berne, P.; Williams, S. K. :	*Dreams and Spiritual Growth,* Paulist Press 1984.
	Dream Symbol Work, Paulist Press 1991.
Sobrino, Jon:	*Christology at the Crossroads,* Orbis 1978.
Teilhard de Chardin:	*The Divine Milieu,* Harper Perennial 2001.
	Hymn of the Earth, Harper Torchbooks 1965.
	Christianity and Evolution, Mariner Books 2002.
Therese of Lisieux:	*The Story of a Soul,* Paraclete Press 2010.
	Collected Letters of St. Therese of Lisieux, Kessinger Publishing 2007.
Thomas Aquinas	*Summa Theologiae,* Cambridge University Press 2006.
Underhill, Evelyn:	*Mysticism,* Book Jungle 2007.
Welch, John:	*Spiritual Pilgrims,* Paulist Press 1982.
Wink, Walter:	*The Powers That Be,* Gallilee Books 19998.
	Engaging The Powers, Augsburg Fortress 1992.
Yungblut, John:	*The Gentle Art of Spiritual Guidance,* Vega Books 2002.

Index